# STUDENT

AF351750

# STUDENT

## 7 Pillars of Strong Foundation

*Authored by*

MAHIPAL SINGH

**Penman** Books

Office No. 303, Kumar House Building,
D Block, Central Market, Opp PVR Cinema,
Prashant Vihar, Delhi 110085, India
Website: www.penmanbooks.com
Email: publish@penmanbooks.com

First Published by Penman Books 2019
Copyright © Mahipal Singh 2019
All Rights Reserved.

Title: Student
Price: ₹249 | $ 9.99
ISBN: 978-93-89024-23-4

No part of this book may be reproduced or transmitted in any form whatsoever, electronic, or mechanical, including photocopying recording, or by any informational storage or retrieval system without the expressed written, dated and signed permission from the author.

LIMITS OF LIABILITY/DISCLAIMER OF WARRANTY: The author and publisher of this book have used their best efforts in preparing this material. The author and publisher make no representation or warranties with respect to the accuracy, applicability or completeness of the contents. They disclaim any warranties (expressed or implied), or merchantability for any particular purpose. The author and publisher shall in no event be held liable for any loss or other damages, including but not limited to special, incidental, consequential, or other damages. The information presented in this publication is compiled from sources believed to be accurate, however, both the publisher and author assume no responsibility for errors or omissions. The information in this publication is not intended to replace or substitute professional advice. The strategies outlined in this book may not be suitable for every individual, and are not meant to provide individualized advice or recommendations.

The advice and strategies found within may not be suitable for every situation. This work is sold with the understanding that neither the author nor the publisher are held responsible for the results accrued from the advice in this book.

All disputes are subject to Delhi jurisdiction only.

# Preface

Books are the very loyal and true friends of students. There is no friend as loyal as a book. I am glad to introduce the book *STUDENT 7- PILLARS OF STRONG FOUNDATION*. Basically the title of the book is prepared to keep in mind for the success of student. I hope this book will be very helpful to you. First of all I am very thankful to all the readers to select this book. It is very important factor to select a good book. I am very thankful to all of my students, friends and my teachers, who help and support me to prepare this book. I can't forget the support of my family, during writing the book how much they sacrifice with my time. I am very thankful to Sh. Deepak Shakya, editor of the book who make the book so beautiful with his amazing editing & skill.

At last but not least I am very thankful to the publication team the *Penman Books* specially MR. TARUN KUMAR SINGH who make my dream true.

All the suggestions and Advice are acceptable.

With regards<br>
*Mahipal Singh*<br>
(*Author*)

# *Foreword*

It is my great pleasure to give foreword and appreciation for the self-help *book* **STUDENT 7 pillars of strong foundation,** which is a definite outcome of teaching, training, counseling and coaching experience of **Mr. Mahipal Singh** author of the book. I know him personally from last 15years. He is very hard working, creative and energetic man. ***Mr. Mahipal Singh*** has about 18 years of multidimensional expertise of teaching and training, coaching and counseling in various organizations. In this period, he mentored thousands of the students enable to help to achieve their life goal, and counseling lot of students about their life goals. He wrote and published 10 subjective books, which are very demandable in the markets.

Parents are the first and most influential teachers for any child in this World. Child's education is most likely an area of great interest to all the parents and they want to provide the best available education to their children. However due to lack of awareness many parents are not aware the opportunities today's changing World. Before going to select the career of the child it is the duty of the parents and teachers to know the strength, interest and weakness and learning style of the individual. In today's dynamic World, ***learning is more important than knowledge.*** Learning style of individual is different but it play very-very important role in our life. The book ***STUDENT 7 pillars of strong foundation*** is a self-help motivational book for students, parents and teachers. It helps to understanding the basics but mandatory steps are to be adopted and implemented by the students to achieve their desired goals at desired time. All the topics covered in the book are written in very simple and clear language. The techniques mentioned in the book are so simplified that everyone can understand and learn without any pre-required knowledge. Once you read these 7-pillars, you will be the masters of your mind and actions.

This book will not only help to your present life, it also helps you find the way to accomplish yours goals in a time bound manner.

**I wish the author all the very best in all his future endeavors.**

**Anil D. Shiwale**
*Training Officer*
*National Skill Training Institute Mumbai*
*Ministry of Skill Development and Entrepreneurship*
*Mumbai Maharashtra India*

# Ackowledgement

Each student is always connected with education, subject, exams and success etc. In his student's life he makes the foundation of his upcoming life. Time used in student's life is decided either he will be ordinary or extraordinary in his family, and society. During this time he faces many attractive things, entertainment, and many more unproductive things. Due to premature mind and nearest environment he faces many problem to take the right decision at right time. Most of the students face these things.

This book is written for all the students whatever their school level, collage, universities or research also. Basically this is a self-help book which will help you to get your aim of life. In this book I try to tell you the simple, important and useful pillars for student's success. I hope this book will help you to make your life success at a desired path. In this book I have describe the importance of student life's decision which will play very important role in their future life.

Here in the book ***STUDENT 7-PILLARS OF STRONG FOUNDATION"*** the abbreviation of student which is describe in very useful and motivated way. These 7- pillars are very useful and adoptable by all the students for a strong foundation of life. These seven pillars are as-

- S- Self-Confidence

- T- Time Management

- U- Uniqueness

- D- Discipline

- E- Energetic

- N- Never Lazy

- T- True Friend

Actually these are the simple and basic important requirements by the students in their success path. All above are always use in every Person's life. But here in my point of view actually life is start with their student's life.

S-  Self-Confidence, in the respect of student, he/she should be self-confident.

T-  Time Management, in the respect of student, his/her time should be managed.

U-  Uniqueness, in the respect of student , he/she is unique in this planet.

D-  Discipline, in the respect of student, he/she should be disciplined.

E-  Energetic, in the respect of student, he/she should always be energetic.

N-  Never Lazy, in the respect of student, he/she never be lazy.

T-  True Friend, in the respect of student, he/she should be true friend.

The author as an teacher see and feel student's life struggle on daily basis. Lot of the students ask me the success mantra and rules to be followed in student's life. I try to give the answer of that question as according to my knowledge but I think it not enough. I read biography of lot of legends of the history who become successfull and popular in the word in the lack of even basic requirements of livelihood. The biography of the legends of the history i.e. Swami Vivekananda, Dr. APJ Abdul Kalam, Dr. B.R Ambedkar, Nelson Mandela and many more. They motivate me and guide me how to help the students at on my own way. So I decide to write a book which can make the light on their life's path. The book *STUDENT 7- PILLARS FOR STRONG FOUNDATION* is to be the real and true friend of you. As states above the  7- pillars, here in this book the author tell about the importance of all these and also tell how they can be accomplished. Here in the book the author use the appropriate real and motivated  stories also which are very helpful to understand the basic concept as per the content. In short I promise you if you understand the values and importance of these said 7- pillars and adopt the policy to implement in every field of life you definitely get the aim of your life.

All the Best.
**Mahipal Singh**
*Author | Teacher*

# A Student's Prayer

O God, source of all wisdom
That, I am a student.

Enlighten my mind.
And strengthen my will.

During  these years of my study,
Assist me in performing  my duties.

Help me preserve in my endeavor,
Till I reach  my goal.

Help me live in your presence.
And behave honorably

Choosing to do, what is right
And pleasing in your sight.

May I always respect my parents.
And kind to the weak And Needy.

Bless me
And all who take special interest

In my growth
Thank you for your love and care me

**(STUDENT)**

# *A to Z Success*

A - Avoid Bad Company.

B - Books Are The Real And True Friends Forever.

C - Character Is What You Are In the Dark.

D - Discipline Is The Refining Fire By Talent Becomes Abilities.

E - Education Is The Chief-Defense Of Our Self And Our Nation.

F - Failure Are The Greatest Teachers.

G - Give More Than You Get.

H - Honesty Is The First Chapter Of The Book Of Wisdom.

I - Impossible Itself Says I Am Possible.

J - Just Don't Give Up Trying To Do What You Really Want To Do.

K - Know What You Want.

L - Learning is The Unique Earning.

M - Make Yourself Self-Start Not Starts By Others.

N - Never Try To Be Appear What You Are Not.

O - Obedience Is Primary Object Of All Sound Education.

P - Punctuality Is The Sign Of Great Man.

Q - Question Provide Key To Unlock Our Unlimited Potential.

R - Respect Measured By Character Not By Money.

S - Save When You Are Young Spend When You Are Old.

T - Tomorrow Never Come, Faith In Today Only.

U - Unite We Stand, Divide We Fall.

V - Vision Is The Art Of Seeing Invisible Things.

W - Work Hard Never Goes Waste.

X - Xerox Not Accepted Originality Always Helpful.

Y - Yield not be discourage.

Z - Zig-Zag Ways Are The Sign Of Big Success.

# Book as a Companion

I have a message for the young and old,

Always have books as companions.

Books were always my friends since last more.

Than 50 years books gave me dreams .

Dreams resulted in missions.

Books helped  me to take up the mission confidently .

Good books for me were angles. they  gave me courage, at

The time of failures and touched my heart gently at
the time of success.

Hence, I ask young friends to have books as a friends.

Books are your great friends.

My home library is the greatest

Beautiful song and greatest

Wealth of my life.

**(Dr. APJ Abdul Kalam)**

# Contents

# One

## Self-Confidence

*The ability or the belief to believe in yourself, to accomplish any task, no matter what are the odds, no matter what are the difficulties, no matter what is the adversity. The belief that you can accomplish it is Self-Confidence.*

Self-confidence is the key to success for everybody in the whole Universe. It is the trust of one's belief or trust in own abilities. Confidence is a feeling of trust in someone or something.

Swami Vivekananda says about self-confidence –"**The ideal of faith in ourselves is the greatest help to us**". What differs man to man is only self-confidence and nothing else. What makes the one man great & successful and another weak & incapable is only "*self- confidence*."

So the self-confidence plays very important role in student's life. Without confidence, nobody can achieve anything which he desires. Student without confidence can't fulfill his dreams. Confidence can only help you to take in the World with more energy and determination, results better knowledge & grades.

Self-confident people usually can influence other people more easily as well as control their own emotions and behaviors more responsibly.

Self-confidence is freedom of doubt; belief in yourself and in your abilities. Many people lack the self-confidence and self-esteem needed to live a happy and healthy life. Self-Esteem is a confidence and satisfaction in oneself. These two things must be present in people's daily lives in order for them to believe that they have the ability to do everything. At this point in my life, I am trying to gain the esteem I need to truly and be happy. The best way to gain self–confidence is to look deep inside of yourself and believe that you have the ability to overcome all obstacles and challenges that you are faced with, on a daily bases, because our self-esteem is one of the few things that we have control.

Self–confidence is something that cannot be taught. It is up to the individual to decide how much belief that they possess inside of themselves. I am at the point where I realize that I must first believe in myself before others will believe in me. Nobody teaches us to be happy or sad. These are natural feelings that come along as we develop mentally, physically, emotionally and psychologically.

When you get to the point where you allow others to dictate how you feel about life, you have to stop and do an internal search. Ask yourself if your lack of self-confidence and self-assurance is holding you back from being the best that you can possibility be. Most often these feeling come from people allowing the negativity of other people to overcome them. You have to be willing to take control of your life and whatever is holding you back. So often we, as a people, look for the validation from society before we validate ourselves. I have allowed society to determine how I should look, dress and feel. It is time for me to take stand and be in control of my own destiny.

## How to build up Self-Confidence

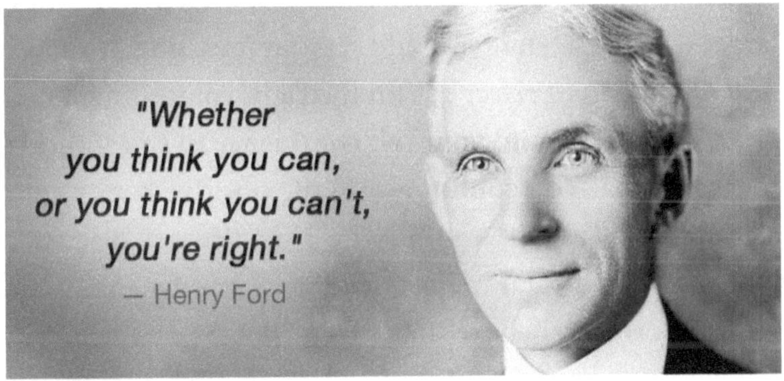


When you fail to achieve your objectives, it is easy to believe that we don't have the ability or you are not enough. However the difference between the success and failure is rarely any lasting ability. You may lack of necessary skill at moment but you can learn that things you needed. The biggest factor is determining your level of success is only your *Self-Confidence.* 'Henry Ford' said "*Whether you believe that you can or you believe that you can't ;you are right*". So the self-confidence is the most important tool for every success. If you want to achieve your goals and objectives, you must have enough self-confidence to see the job thoroughly. As the size of your goals and ambition grows, your level of self- confidence must grow to match it.

You know the mountaineers who just includes confidence and they do wonders. What is the secret? How can they are so positive about their self? The good news it that is only confidence says self-confidence. But the self-confidence is not happen by accident. It comes from repeated practice and small successes which build into large successes. Here we add the famous line "*Practice Makes The Man Perfect*". With the right commitment and efforts, you can build your self confidence in short period of time and as you continue with the positive habits your self-confidence will continue to grow. Here I discuss a true story of a Mountaineer Padma Shree Dr. Arunima Sinha she totally believe in the fact, "*Believe and Achieve*".

Arunima Sinha ( Born 20 July 1988) is the first female amputee to scale *Mount Everest.* She was a National level volleyball player who was pushed from the the running train by some robbers in the year 2011 while she was resisting them. As a result one of her lags had to be amputated below the knee. While still being treated in

AIIMS, she decide to climb *Mount Everest*. She excelled in the basic mountaineering courses from various institutes. She contacted Bachendri Pal, the first woman to climb *Mount Everest* in 2011 telephonically and signed up for training under her. Finally after two and half year (approx.) she completed her summited of Mount Everest at 10:55am on 21 may 2013.So here *she believes and she achieve.*

*Her aim was to climb all the continents highest peaks and hoist the National flag of India. She has already done six peaks by 2014 Everest in Asia, Kilimanjaro in Africa, Elbrus in Europe, Kosciuszko in Australia, Aconcagua in Argentina and Carstensz Pyramid (Pancakes Jaya ) in Indonesia. She completed her final summit of Mount Vinson in Antarctica on 4 January 2019.*

So the self-confidence is the most important tool for everyone whether you are a student, sportsman, mountaineer, politician or any others.

*"IT IS THE SELF-CONFIDENCE YOU BELIEVE AND YOU ACHIEVE"*

No matter what kind of work you do, you can strive to do your best at it. When you know that you have given your best to the task, you know that you could not have given anymore. This allows to you feels relaxed and more confident about with friends, family, classmates and your institutes/schools which enable you to receive positive confidence, building *self-confidence*. Here are some requirements which are mendatary to build up self-confidence within you.

## Attitude

The attitude of a person towards life is deciding factor in his life. How a man perceive the events of his life and how he react to them is important. Whenever a glass is half full or half empty depend on the attitude of a person looking at it. A pessimist says half of the glass is empty and a optimist says half glass filled with water. True fact is half filled with water while half filled with air. Never focus on the empty glass. If you constantly focus on what is not

done; you will move into the negative state of mind. So mind your attitude. Be aware what remains to be done but at the same time appreciate what has been done and keep adding to it.

As a student it is not a matter how much you are busy and it is not enough to be busy, so as ants. The real question is, what are you busy about? Don't count the number of hours you study, count the concept/chapters and amount of understanding you are filling each hours with. So totally we can say attitude is a little thing which makes the huge difference. Nothing can stop the man with the right mental attitude from achieving his goal; nothing on the earth can help you with the wrong mental attitude.

Just because you are right, does not mean, I am wrong. You just haven't seen life from my side.

Don't afraid to ask the questions to your teachers. Remember one thing; if you ask the questions and other can laugh at you, you become a fool for a moment. But if you don't ask, you remain fool for your whole life, you only choose which is better and effective. So the attitude from the student perspective is the mindset that you carry. Attitude is equally important as ability. Every problem has a solution, only if we can change our *ATTITUDE*. We can try to understand the role of attitude simply as on the number of the English alphabets…

$$H+A+R+D+W+O+R+K$$

$$8+1+18+4+23+15+18+11= 98\%$$

$$K+N+O+W+L+E+D+G+E$$

$$11+14+15+23+12+5+4+7+5= 96\%$$

$$L+U+C+K$$

$$12+21+3+11= 47\%$$

$$M+O+N+E+Y$$

$$13+15+14+5+25 =72\%$$

$$A+T+T+I+T+U+D+E$$

$$1+20+20+9+20+21+4+5= 100\%$$

***It is therefore our attitude towards life and work that makes our life 100% successful.***

It is very much known to us two persons can view the same incident in different ways. But the important thing is how we learn a lesson from this paradox. The world is a mirror we find that what we ourselves project is reflected back to us. As we look at it its looks back at us. There is nothing absolutely good or absolutely bad. What is good for one may not good for another. What is good for one occasion may not good for another occasion. The idea is that value changes as per situation and the person's concerned. But this should became a reason to make circumstances an excuse for the happiness or unhappiness of an individual. Circumstances should be understood properly. Your attitude is everything towards any stage or any situation of life. A student's attitude is basic fundamental to be succeed. Attitude is what makes the difference in the things. Attitude is a manner of thinking, feeling, or behaving that reflect the state of mind not only the current state of life but your future state of life as well.

## Will Power

For all the stories of successes and failures in people's life there are different reasons. But in every successful person's life one factor is inevitably common and that is **will power.** The amount of success a man achieves in his life can be gauged by the amount of will power he cultivated. Mountains can also be moved from their place only by the *Will Power*.

Will power itself is a compound of our self (ego) and our mind – it is the positive and creative function of our mind, which impels us along a particular course of action and enables us to do our chosen activities in a definite way. It is the power of the mind which enables us to do what we know to be right, and desist from doing what we know to be wrong. Will power is the common factor of success in any work. We may say that studying for an exam requires a different kind of efforts that preparing for hurdle race, one key factor in any achievement is will power. Without this will power, a student will not be able to motivate himself/herself to study long hours nor will an athlete be prepared to spend long hours training in the Sun. The degree of success varies in the proportion to will power. In fact, this is true of any endeavor, even in the field of spiritual development, without will power self-development or improvement is impossible-this is simple but hundred percent true. In the absence of will power, all talents, qualities and endeavors come to nothing.

We commit errors and face tragedies in life because the lack of will power. We know what is good for us will help in progress but we unable to find the strength to pursue such course of action. We know that what harmful for us and what we should avoid, yet we are unable to avoid such actions. For examples a doctor know the harmful effects of drinking alcohol and smoking. Yet he can't give up his addiction. This is only of the lack of will power. So the question is how we will improve our will power? It is very important question everybody's life, specially for the student because student life is the first and very important battle field to know the importance of will power and how to increase it.

## First start with simple exercise

1. Skip one meal one day every week. Instead, take some substitute in the beginning. Later on, this substitute should also be stopped.

2. Once in a week, practice silence for half a day. Spend the time in reading self-help books or meditating, if you are habitual to meditation. Avoid unnecessary thinking too. Self-talk you can. Don't sleep away at that time. It is not silence.

3. Once a week skip taking tea or coffee if you have a habit. But don't resort to another bad habit to keep up this practice. For example if you go to the cinema in order to skip a mental or practice silence, it is a very bad idea.

You can take the help of your friends who are interested in your welfare. Without their help it may be difficult to achieve the goal single handedly. Beware not all are friends. They may disturb your vow !

Moreover, eagerly await the day of practice ! Prepare the mind from day before, so that you will find it is easy to control the mind. And once you have, compliment yourself with some treat. I am not joking, it will work.

Our mind is like a child, we have to do something to keep it obedient. The mind is like a white cloth. The white cloth can take whatever colour it is dipped in. Similarly mind also can take suggestions and ideas. By giving good and strong ideas we can promote it well and make stronger.

## Sense of Humour

Take two joke-pills and call me in the morning ! That is the prescription of many physicians and psychologist who believe you can laugh your way to health. Today's healers offer succinct advise; don't take your life too seriously; it is temporary.

There are the occasions, some situations, where you can't decide what to tell or how to react to the situation. There is however a warning beware; humour may be dangerous to your illness! The mental but eventually it will heal most of your physical illness also. Because now it is an established fact that mental health and physical health are inter connected. In many cases it is the mind that control the body.

For every event there is a lighter side. We fail to look at it. But if we can look at the lighter side, many problems won't arise at all. Things will be eased out. On many occasions, a witty answer would be better than a serious explanative answer.

All of us know Abraham Lincoln, he was taller than average Americans. Once somebody want to tease him and ask what should be the correct length of the leg's of you. Lincoln answered from the waist to floor! This silenced the questioner. This is one example of a great sense of humour.

Swami Vivekananda also had face the same situation in America. There were many misconception about India in that country due to the propaganda of Christian Missionaries there. He was asked by someone, Why do mothers throw the babies to crocodile in your country? Swami Vivekananda answered, because it is easier for them to chew ! You see, there can be no use of arguing under such circumstances. Looking at the humour side of the situation is very useful to such occasions. So the sense of humour is equally important in student life. Actually it encourage the atmosphere to openness.

## Character

When wealth is lost, nothing is lost. When health is lost something is lost; when character is lost everything is lost. The mental and moral qualities differentiate to an individual. Neither money plays, nor name, nor fame, nor learning; it is Character that can cleave through adamantine walls of difficulties.

If you really want to judge the character of a man, don't look at his great performances. Every fool may become a hero at one time or another. Watch a man do his most common actions; those are indeed the things which will tell you the real character of a great man.

# Power of concentration

The main difference between man and the animals is their power of concentration. All success in any field of life specially student life is the result of this i.e. power of concentration. Everybody knows the something about concentration. We see its results every day. High achievements in arts, music, writing, teaching, business and study etc. are the results of concentration. An animal has very little power of concentration. Those who have trained animals find much difficulty in the fact that the animal is constantly forgetting what is told him. Herein is the difference between man and animal is that man has a greater power of concentration. The difference in their power of concentration also constitutes the difference between man and man. The difference is the degree of concentration.

Everybody's mind becomes concentrated at times. We all concentrate upon those things we love, and we love those things upon which we concentrate our mind. Concentration is the ability to focus the attention on one single thought or subject, excluding everything else from the field of awareness. A trained mind is able to focus, without being distracted by thoughts, noises or anything else.

## The Importance of Concentration

The ability to focus the mind is one of the most important abilities one should possess. Why do you need to be able to focus your mind? It is a skill that helps in all walks of life, to study, read, work, drive, get tasks done, meditate, and for everything else.

## Self-Talk

To build the self-confidence self-talk is a very compulsory. Where you spend most of the time? Is it with yours friends, with yours family or somewhere else? Answer is that you spend most of time only with yourself. So being a student it is extremely important that you continue talk to yourself with positive and healthy attitude. Let's take two situation as:-

When you are going to appear in your exams, you feel yourself suppressed by a the pressure; a psychological stress occupies in your mind. The last few weeks before exams are very crucial and unfortunately that is also the time when the doubts develops. The self doubts hampers the productivity, lowers the motivation, impact the rhythm of the students in those crucial days. So it important that you talk to yourself positively in such crucial times. Self-Talk gives you the great motivation, idea to solve inner doubts. Most of the successful personality on this planet are great thinkers. Every problem have a solution but we have to think how it is to be solve. So self talk gives you right and perfect way to solve any of the problem and it also help you make the path for the journey of success. As you know the two motivation i.e. internal and external. External motivation is temporary but internal is permanent. Self-Talk is the exercise for the internal motivation.

And second, if the student fails somehow, he takes the failure so seriously that he lost his natural style and ability to concentrate not prepare well for the next exams. You must in order to ensure a healthy and receptive frame of mind, do a positive self-talk.

Many people think that they need to have confidence before they can commit themselves fully to everything they do. That is putting the cart before the horse.

You need to give your best effort each time and learn from your outcomes. You will then see that your best continues to get better each-time. This continuous improvement ensures that your self-confidence is regularly reinforced.

## The Killer Action to Boost Self-Confidence

1. *You must say goodbye to negativity.*

2. *You must always think positive and creative.*

3. *You must act positively.*

4. *You should say goodbye to negative people.*

5. *You should make the clear goals.*

6. *You should groom yourself.*

7. *You should speak truth over yourself.*

8. *You should read motivational book.*

9. *You should ready to learn.*

10. *You should be responsible.*

11. *You should be appear confident.*

12. *You should be creative.*

13. *You should make the plans.*

14. *You should have a friendly personality.*

15. *You should have a good moral* character.

16. You should develop your will power.

17. You should be honest to yourself &others.

18. You should speaks truth over yourself.

19. Believe in hard work not in shortcuts.

20. You should be punctual.

# Self-Confidence check-up

**Direction: Rate from 0 to 10 how much you believe each statement. '0' means you do not believe it at and '10'means you completely it.**

### Statement Rating

1.  I believe in myself ____________
2.  I am just as valuable as other people ____________
3.  I would rather be me than someone else ____________
4.  I am proud of my accomplishments ____________
5.  I feel good when I get compliments ____________
6.  I can handle criticism ____________
7.  I feel good at solving problems ____________
8.  I love trying new things ____________
9.  I respect myself ____________
10.  I like the way I look ____________
11.  I love myself even when others reject me ____________
12.  I know my positive qualities ____________
13.  I focus on my successes and not my failures ____________
14.  I'm not afraid to make mistakes ____________
15.  I am happy to be me ____________

Total score _________

Overall, how would you rate your self-esteem on the following scale:

0_________________________________________________10

I completely dislike who I am like who I am what would need to change in order for you to move up one point on the rating scale?

(i.e. for example, if you rated yourself a "6" what would need to happen for you to be at a"7"?)

# Two

## Time Management

***Time is more valuable than money you can get,***
***more money, but you cannot get more time.***

Time management is the co-ordination of tasks and activities of an individual's. Essentially, the purpose of time management is enabling people to get more and better work done in less time. Time management is the process of planning And exercising conscious control of time spend on specific activities, especially to increase effectiveness efficiency or productivity. A management system is a designed combination of process, tools, techniques and methods. Time management is very important for everybody. Being a student, time management is most important. Student life is a life of dreams. Without management of time nobody can fulfill their dreams and goals. Good time management will increase effectiveness and productivity. It is the most important tool to improve Individual, society and Nation also.

Time management is the managing of your time so that time is used to your advantage and it gives you a chance to speed up your most valuable resource in the way you choose.

Time management is an endless series of small and large decisions that gradually changes the shape of your life

No one has total control over a daily schedule. Someone always will make demands. However everyone has some control and probably more than they realize. Even within structured time, there are the opportunities to select which tasks or activities to handle at what time and what priority to that task.

Managing one's time is an self-struggle for anyone, but especially for student's leadership position. It is important to recognize that time management can help you as long as you are willing to assess what you have been doing and make a commitment to budget your time so better. Take an opportunity to examine what you can do for yourself and make some positive changes to the way that you are run your schedule. I states about time management for myself it is nothing its only self-management only.

Time is precious, because time is limited for everyone in whole World. If you lost your all the money and resources, you can earn again, if you lost your home, you can get it back but once you lost your precious time, it will never come back.

If we want to do something great or want to become a great personality and also want to complete our needs then we need to know and learn about the importance of time and also we need to utilize it.

A successful person wants to utilize more and more use of *24 hours* or a day. He focuse entire routine only, on the best use of time. **Mike Murdoch also said the secret of your future is hidden in your routine.**

Travelling is an important part of our routine. Today every person makes many trips, in which he has a lot of time. The only difference is that while the common person sits on hand during the journey, but the successful person uses the maximum of his precious time. Therefore the best use of time is to make maximum use of travelling time. Mahatma Gandhi used to sleep while travelling so that he would always be refreshed. Edison was so conscious about the waste of time, but in adolescence when he traveled in the train, he used to gather in his experiments. Microsoft founder **Bill Gates** executes this principle by doing important things on mobile during the visit. **Bill Gates** had once set a map of Africa in his garage so that when he stopped the ignition of his car, his intriguing seconds would not be wasted but he would have some use. All successful people are careful about the time, because they know that time is strong. Success is possible only while there is the proper use of time. We can also take advantage of our travelling time. It takes a lot of time for people while travelling from home to work and back to home. Most of the salesman spends their time in travelling. We should know that if we travel for two and a half hour every day, then our life is made a loss about 10% of the time in the journey, you can make it a meaningful use of time while doing some valuable work. Look, most of the people either listening songs on mobile, read newspapers or keep chuckling during the journey. They do not know that by reading motivational books, listening to academic tapes or doing any other important work they can reach their goals more quickly. Studies have shown that 45% of the students usually passed in the working hours with a non-productive way. Nobody likes to wait, many times we are compelled to wait for a person, bus or train. Therefore, we should have list of such scattered tasks that we can handle when we are waiting. If we are prepared for short work in our bags, then we will not even have to wait and our work will also happen. Famous British Astro-Physician "Herman wondi" had travel so many trips that he used to retire his office during the trips. Once upon a time when his flight was delayed at a European airport, they wrote a research paper using the time. *It is called the use of the travel time!*, when you have strong desire to do something in your mind, then time comes. *Remember Fredrick Nietzsche, when a person has a more things to keep, then there are hundred pockets in day dress. So take care of time than time will take care of yourself too.*

## Time Management means Self-Management

The best preparation for good work tomorrow is to do good work today. It is saying that **Time is Money** actually it is not a complete truth. It is like as time may called money if you utilize your time effectively and this you can earn money. On the other way if you do not utilize your time effectively you can't earn a single coin. Time is money only for those who can cash it.

We all have a bank named *time*. Every morning it credit 86400 seconds in our account. Every night it debit the seconds which are not used for an important work. At that time you have no balance and time don't give to you any overdrive facilities. Every morning it open your account again destroyed night remaining time. If you are fail to use that time, it is hour's lose. We can't go back in time and not demand for extra time. You have keep yourself to your today deposit only.

Time is as a precise thing, which is realized only after lost. Time in past and future is waste. Time is valuable at this very moment only. So live, utilize and enjoy the present moment. So the time utilization is important secret of success.

Time don't not wait for anybody. Therefore don't waste the time for negative and paining things. If you use the present time effectively for making your desired future you will definitely success. In point of time management for the students the Pareto Law is very useful.

## Pareto Law

In order to succeed in the exams, hard work is not only solution. You ought to work smart, study smart, think smart. After meet the numbers of toppers and successful student I realize that they does smart study. So the main question is what is smart study? They use plenty of technique for smart study but mostly they use Pareto Law.

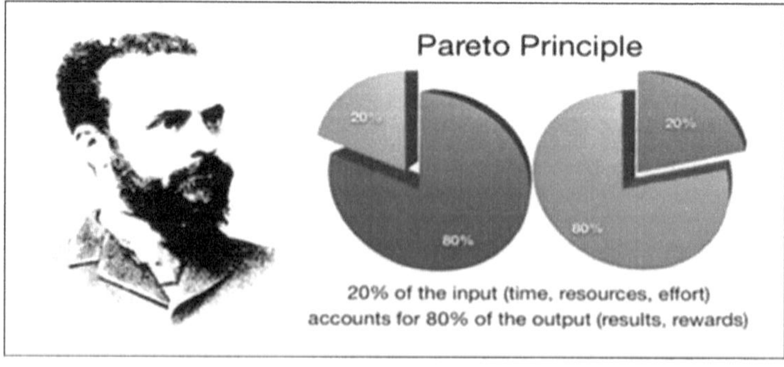

In 1906, Italian economist Vilfredo Pareto was taking a leisurely stroll in his garden. He was examining his pea plants, and he noticed a pattern 20% of the pea pods contained 80% of the peas. He developed a mathematical model for this pattern, and he produced what is now known as the Pareto Principle, or the 80/20 rule. This causal relationship is rooted in the fact that 80% of the effects come from 20% of the causes. Pareto then applied his model to land ownership in Italy, and he determined that 80% of the land was owned by 20% of the people. A modern day example of this can be found at the root of the wealth distribution of many nations, where 80% of the wealth is controlled by 20% of the people. While the Pareto principle is an economics theory, it can be applied to your life at school and help you improve your performance by optimizing your time use.

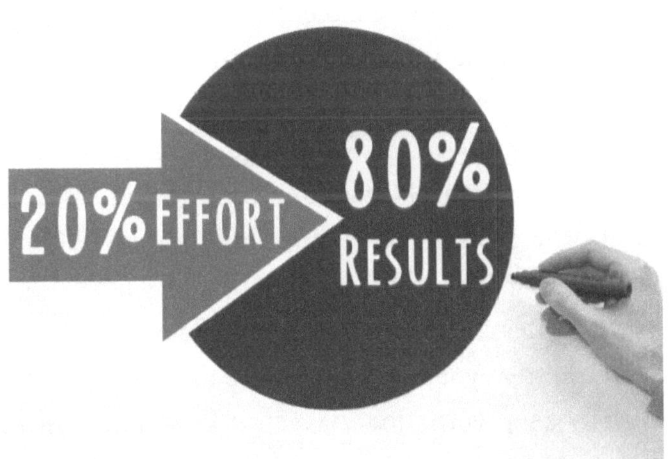

If you apply the Pareto Principle to one of the keys of academic success, studying, you will find that you get 80% of your studying done in 20% of your time actually spent studying. This might sound shocking at first, but bear with me for a moment. Think to when you're studying: you spend a lot of time being distracted, re-reading, thinking about other things, day dreaming about your future, or you leave to go grab a coffee. Let's take a 5 hour study session at the library and break it down:

20% of 5 hours is 1 hour, so in theory, you only need 1 hour of studying to achieve 5 hours of "studying". The rest of the time will be spent on your phone, waiting in line for coffee, checking Facebook or another website, or simply zoning out in moments of lost focus. Starting to make sense?

Let's attach this to a different example of not so near future; you are now in the process of starting your own business. The Pareto Principle predicts that 80% of your business will come from 20% of your customers. This is why as a business owner, it is imperative that you work harder initially to retain your regular client base than worry about complaints from one-time customers, as they will not provide as much business as your core 20% will. How large that 20% will become is up to your skills and abilities in sales and marketing, but the fact remains is that you want to treat your best customers the best, as they will essentially keep you afloat based on how much business they provide for you. This is why many companies employ a VIP system or preferred client program; they understand the value of a regular customer.

While the Pareto Principle itself is hardly cutting edge (I mean, it has been around for over 100 years), the applications to which it can be applied are always changing. In today's world, there are so many outlets for our energy, and we simply have to learn how to harness this energy to make the best use of the 80/20 ratio.

The first way to do this is to not over-indulge all of your time in one thing; diversify your portfolio, so to speak. So instead of spending your entire day studying, break up your day into a variety of activities, otherwise you'll simply be damning yourself from the beginning to accomplish less. Divide your day into smaller chunks of time in which to accomplish your goals for that day. Keep your mind fresh by constantly changing things up.

For example, let's say that you have to study for two midterms, have an essay due, and also have some routine homework to accomplish, and let's say it's all due in a week's time. Instead of stressing about one thing over the other, allocate a balanced amount of time to each until you accomplish the task. Maximize that 20% of your time each day to achieve 80% of your work. Keep things changing to limit distractions and other contributing factors to the wasted 80% of your time. By managing your 80% "waste time" effectively, you can accomplish 80% of multiple things in the same time as you would normally have accomplished 80% of only one thing.

Our brain traditionally gets bored of doing one thing after only half an hour to an hour, so by changing up the activity, you're essentially resetting the clock on the 20% of your time to accomplish 80% of a new thing. This is also why I've always lived by the philosophy that I'm more productive when I'm busier and mildly stressed about how jam-packed my day is. Perhaps you've noticed this too: if you have extended periods of down time, despite all that available time to accomplish whatever tasks you have on hand, you in fact accomplish less because of the lack of motivation, the lack of urgency, and natural tendency to procrastinate. If you want maximize the benefits of the Pareto Principle, simply do more things and manage accordingly.

So with the coming exam season, during your day-to-day routine at work, or your next work-out, try to introduce a bit more variety into it to reset the 80/20 clock and invigorate your mind to accomplish more in the set amount of time you have each day. Each task will feel fresh and fun, your motivation to accomplish things will increase since your list is more challenging, and you'll accomplish more things in a more efficient manner. This article is living proof that the 80/20 principle works. I wrote it in about 25 minutes in class when my mind started wandering from the course material.

**Ask the importance of time from followings:**

1. *Ask one year importance who fail in exams.*

2. *Ask one month importance the newborn baby's mother.*

3. *Ask the one week importance, weekly magazine editor.*

4. *Ask the one hour importance who wait to meet his/her lover.*

5. *Ask one minute importance whose train/flight left.*

6. *Ask the one second importance, who saved from accident.*

7. *Ask the importance of millisecond, who comes runner up in Olympics.*

*Do not waste your time that thing which gives you sorrows and pain. Expand your time with those who want to see you successful not with negative peoples. Use every moment hundred percent.*

> **Knowing is not enough; we must apply**
> **Willing is not enough; we must do.**

## What are the time waste factors:

1. *Lack of planning.*

2. *Lack of priorities.*

3. *Lack of goals and objectives.*

4. *Over commitment.*

5.  *Unrealistic time estimates.*

6.  *Attempting too much in too little time.*

7.  *Fear of the consequence of a mistake.*

8.  *Enjoyment of socializing [Facebook, WhatsApp etc.]*

9.  *Lack of confidence in the facts.*

10.  *Broad interest.*

## 101 Time Management & Time Saver Strategies

1.  Define your objectives.

2.  Set the priorities.

3.  Clarify your values.

4.  Set goals that are specific.

5.  Set the goals that are measurable.

6.  Set the goal that are realistic.

7.  Work on top priorities.

8.  Before action make plan.

9.  Develop action plans based on goals.

10.  Record and evaluate how you spend the time.

11.  Combine the activities.

12.  Ensure that daily, weekly & long term goals are congruent with your values.

13.  Catch the time watchers.

14.  Be flexible.

15. Have a little task in hands.

16. Review the lecture notes soon after the lecture.

17. Review lecture notes throughout the term.

18. Do not rely on cramming for exams.

19. Remember work expands to fill the time available.

20. Percent of what you do yields 80 percent of the result.

21. 80 Percent of what you do yields 20 percent of the result.

22. Let your subconscious work for- starts papers and creative work early.

23. Keep a note pad at all times.

24. Take Leaning skill workshop.

25. Have a purpose for everything you do.

26. Set goals that include a specified time frame for completion.

27. Make to do lists.

28. Break big task into short projects.

29. Do the hard tasks first.

30. Eliminate tasks you do not have to do yourself.

31. Work on top priorities.

32. Break down big tasks into short projects.

33. Do the hard tasks first.

34. Eliminate tasks you do not have to do yourself.

35.  Complete one task before starting another.

36.  Delegate the work.

37.  Allow enough time for each task.

38.  Allow extra time for the unexpected

39.  Avoid busyness

40.  Allow time for family, friends and your self

41.  Use calendars; term, week, daily.

42.  Set deadlines.

43.  Consolibate discretionary time in blocks.

44.  Do creative work where you will not be disturbed.

45.  Communicate clearly the first time.

46.  Get feedback on your communications.

47.  Do not over schedule.

48.  Know your limitations.

49.  Use the telephone or email.

50.  Group phone calls, emails together.

51.  Return calls at a fixed time.

52.  Keep time filler tasks by the phone.

53.  Keep a clean desk.

54.  Do not waste other people's time.

55.  Plan meetings.

56.  Direct meetings purposefully.

57.  Start meetings on time.

58.  Keep meetings on agenda.

59.  Time limit agenda items.

60.  End meetings on time.

61.  Handle mail once.

62.  Throw out what you will not read.

63.  Use a tickler system to remind you of due dates.

64.  Let your family handle guests.

65.  Fix hours for appointments.

66.  Go to the other parson's room or office.

67.  Meet outside of your office.

68.  Block interruptions of appointments.

69.  Do not trust your memory -write it down.

70.  Develop a good life system.

71.  Let someone hold you accountable

72.  Get exercise.

73.  Schedule in more fun.

74.  Take a day off each week.

75.  Learn to say "NO" more often.

76.  Take time to nature for your spirituality.

77.  Remember,today may be your last day.

78.  Take your time.

79.  Accept responsibility for your time.

80.  Strive for a balanced life.

81.  Use the little windows of time.

82.  Group related tasks.

83.  Use your peak times wisely.

84.  Avoid procrastinating.

85.  Plan tasks before starting them.

86.  Narrarate self-discipline & gratification daily.

87.  Narrarate your concentration ability.

88.  Learn memory enhancement techniques.

89.  Develop a procedure manual for future reference.

90.  Learn from failures & mistakes, then forget them.

91.  Review long and short-term goals often.

92.  Eliminate tasks not related to your goals.

93.  Eliminate tasks that interfere with balance.

94.  Reward yourself for effective time management.

95.  Use post-it notes.

96.  Use your Day-Timer.

97.  Give yourself time to relax each day.

98.  Plan ahead to ward off typical distractions.

99.  Learn to make decisions.

100.  Wherever you go, there you are, therefore, be all there.

101.  When you finish something, add it to your "to do" list, then cross it off-it looks good and feels great.

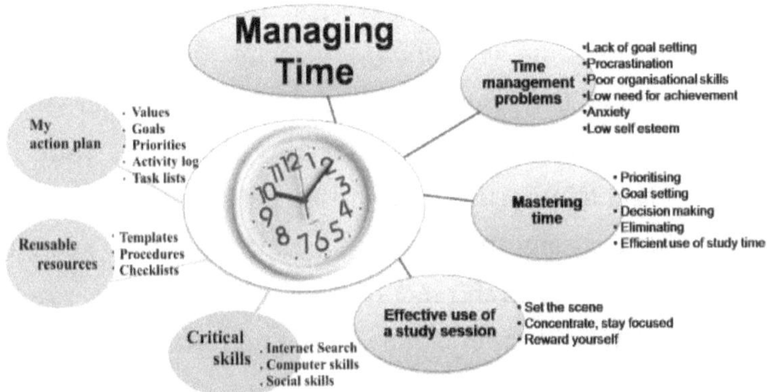


Not all time management methods work for everyone. Understanding who are a student /learner can help you assess which method is best for you. After assessment, choose a time management organizational tool that can you in being more productive time manager.

## Important Techniques to Managing Time

1. Build your schedule around your commitment. Some activities are required fixed time and some flexible.

2. Fixed- classes, eating, organization and coaching/ tution.

   *Flexible- sleeping, study, recreation, personal grooming.*

3. *Plan sufficient study for justice to each subject. Most college classes are planned to require about two hours of outside work per week per credit. By multiplying*

*your credit load by two you can get a good idea of the time you should provide for studying.* Of course, if you are a slow reader, or have other study deficiencies, you may need to plan more time in order to meet the competition from your classmates. Break assignments into smaller segments, such as library research read articles and take notes, rough draft, edit paper, final draft, break study tasks into smaller segments such as- read chapter, outline chapter, make note cards, study note cards, review for exam.

4. Study at a regular time and in a regular place. Establishing habits of regularity in studying is extremely important. Knowing what you are going to study, and when, saves a lot of time in making decisions, finding necessary materials etc. Avoid generalizations is your schedule such as "study". Commit yourself more definitely to "study history" or "study chemistry"etc. at certain hours.

5. Study as soon after class as possible. Check over lecture notes while they are still fresh in your mind. Start assignments while your memory of the assignment is still accurate. Remember, one hour of study immediately after class is probably better than two hours of study a few days later.

6. Utilize off hours for study those scattered one or two hours free period between classes are easily wasted.

Using them for study will result in free time for recreational activities later on.

7.  Study not more than two hours on any one course/ subject at one time. After studying for two hours you begin to tire and your ability to concentrate decrease rapidly. To keep up your efficiency, take a book and then switch to study another subject.

8.  Borrow time don't steal it whenever an unexpected activity arises that takes up time you had planned is studying, decide immediately where you are poor for free time to make up the missed study time and adjust your schedule for that week.

9.  Survey your normal time schedule and analyze it.

10.  Do one thing at a time.

11.  Keep your workplace free from clutter.

12.  Know your goals. Set priorities.

13.  Think before doing

14.  Finish one task before start another.

15.  Schedule your commitment time first (class, work, sports etc.)

16.  Put your objectives on writing.

17.  Maintain regular reading plan.

18.  Break your major goals into sub goals.

19.  Set dead line to yourself.

20.  Take occasional, sharp break.

21.  Reward yourself a completing task /project.

## Benefits of time management

1.  *It help to reduce stress. Managing your time can directly reduce your stress.*

2.  *Get more done, of course, being productive is one of the main goals of time management.*

3.  *Less rework-being organized results less rework and mistake.*

4.  *Improve the productivity*

5.  *Don't go shortcuts.*

6.  *Make your notes in your language's.*

# Three

## *Uniqueness*

Every human being on this planet is unique in his or her dreams, experience, talent and challenges. Everyone is special with unique combinations of abilities and needs that effect of our whole life You are the unique in the universe physically, emotionally, socially and intellectually, so you can not compare to any others. You are unique even if there are common needs and characteristics that particular age or stage development. Every student have a genuine and inborn talent which make him or her differ with others, We must have to find out our inborn talent. Our genuine talent is only thing which differs one to another.

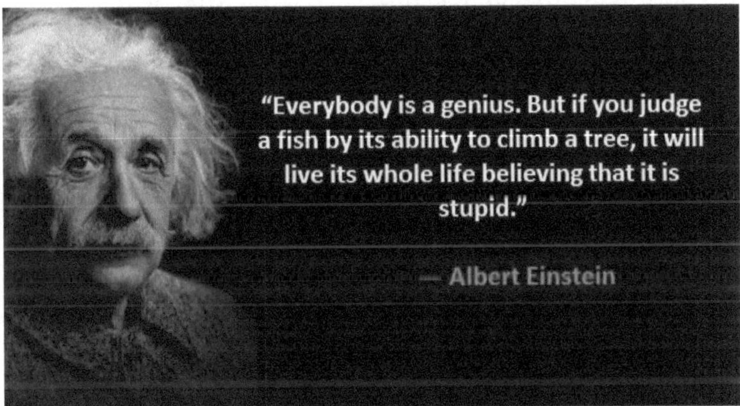


We get uniqueness by birth. We can make our life happier and creative and more productive only by the use of our unique talent. All of us deserve the opportunities to learn in the ways that makes the most of their strength and help them to overcome their weakness.

For examples even in a single grade classroom with 25 to 30 students of age 8 to 9 years will be reading at precisely the same ability level. They will also differ in ways they are able to understand and solve the problem of any particular subject. They will have different personalities -some will be shy, some will be confident, some outgoing, some quite but competent. They each have their own life experiences and feelings about themselves. They have the different likes, dislikes, interest and needs.

However this does not means that a teacher has to prepare 25 to 30 different lesson plans whether it is single grade or multi grade classroom. Instead the teacher must be able to get know and understand each of the students and prepare teaching or learning activities that will respond to reflect these individual needs of students. As students work individuals or independently in small-groups they will benefit in their own way from these activities. If you have a strong desire to know and enhance your talent, you should know yours's learning style. Your learning style is the quality tool which enables you to get it your genuine talent. If you enjoy the every movement of life without any limit of time means what you are doing is your inborn talent that's total meaning is you are enjoying your work or job. So before going more over, we try to understand the individual's learning.

It is generally accepted that there are different learning styles of individual. While most of us fall across the spectrum of each styles. Every student have their unique learning styles. Here we discuss strategies to improve engagement for students of each style.

## Learning Style

Information Enters Your Brain By The Three Main Way:- Seeing, Hearing and Touching, Which One You Use The Most Is Called Your Learning Style. One More Learning Is By Taste But It Is Used In Some Of The Field Like looking. There Are Three Most Of Learners Are:-

### *Visual Learner – Learnt By Sight.*

*Let Me See It !*

### *Auditory Learner - Learnt By Hearing.*

*Let Me Listen It !*

## Kinesthetic Learner – Learn By Touch Or By Doing.

*Let Me Do It !*

## Visual learners:

- Take the numerous detail notes.

- Tend to sit in the front.

- Be neat and clean.

- Often close their eyes to visualize or remember something.

- Find something to watch if getting bored.

- Like to see what they are learning.

- Benefit from illustration and presentation that use too colour.

- Are attract to written or spoken language rich imaginary.

- Prefer to stimulates to be isolated from auditory and kinaesthetic distraction.

- Find passive surroundings ideal.

### Auditory learner:

- He sit where they can hear but need not pay attention to what is happening in front.
- He may not coordinates colour and cloth but can explain what they are wearing and why.
- He hum and talk to themselves or other been boarded.
- He acquire knowledge by reading a loud.
- He remember by verbalising lesion to themselves.

### Kinesthetics learner:

- Need to be active and frequent breaks.
- Speak with their hands and gestures.
- Remember what saw done but have a difficulty to recall what was said or seen.
- Find reasons to thinker or moved when boarded.
- Rely on what they can directly experience or perform.
- Activities like cooking, construction, engineering, art help them perceive and learn.
- Enjoy field trips and task that involve manipulating material.
- Sit near the door and some place else where they can easily get up move and move around.

- He feel uncomfortable in classroom where they lack opportunities of hands on experience.

- Communicates by touching and appreciate physically expressed encouragement.

## You makes you Genius

Look at the history of the world. All those who have achieved something great have done so by means of hard work. They are wholly absorbed in their work. Such work gave them limitless joy and contentment. It inspires them with energy and self-confidence. Thomas Alva Edition, the uncommon genius, with more than two thousands inventions to his credit, said, Inventions are not by accident; they are reward for endless efforts.

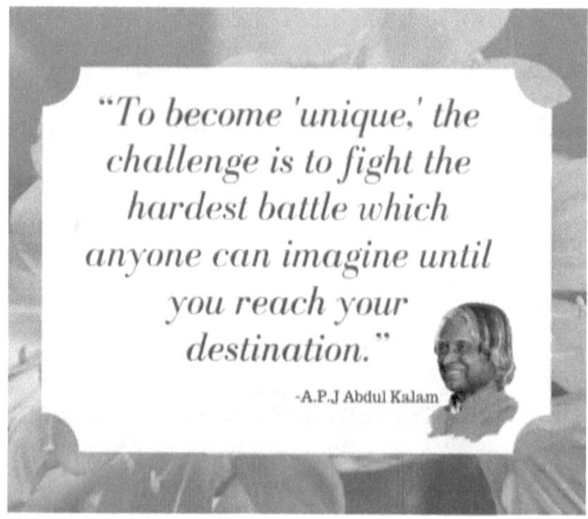


Genius is one percent inspiration and ninety-nine percent perspiration (bath in sweat). Genuine success and unending industry -are inseparable companions. Inspite of hard work one may fail. But without sincere efforts no one can attain excellence. We should remember that we could get valuable objects only by the means of continuous efforts. It is only in the dictionary that "success comes before work".

Take up an idea. Make that idea your life; think of it; dream of it; live on that idea. Let the brain, muscles, nerves, every part of your body be full of that idea, just leave every other idea alone. This is the way to success, This is the way great spiritual giants are produced". And remember the important thought of the great man Swami Vivekanand

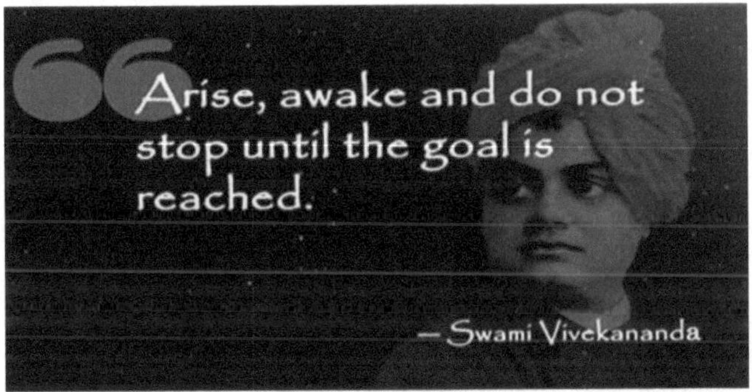


No individual is identical to another. Hence in order to prove ourselves we need not all be eminent scientists. Their zest for work must inspire us to attain excellence in our own fields. Imitation does not make you great; inspiration can be derived from a great person. You are You, You can't be the other.

Indeed we are all different from one another in gait and speech, in interest and aptitude, in skills and abilities. We do not need to imitate anybody. But can we achieve success in the task that we have undertaken? Can we pursue our goal with courage and confidence? Can we overcome unnerving sense of defeatism? Can we drive away our submissiveness, our servitude, and inferiority complex.

Whatever may be the field – religion, arts, literature, or science- highest achievement is possible only by means of incessant effort. All those who have enriched our wealth of knowledge are people who exemplify the importance and glory of hard work. The intensify of their aspiration, the enthusiasm in their work, the concentration of their mind, the height of their success -are these not the source of inspiration for people working in any field? If we want to achieve success in our efforts, we have to take them as our models, we must work with joy and enthusiasm, move on with courage and fervour.

## Passion and creativity

What is needed to be greatness, is your passion and creativity only. This passion should not be limited to the technical aspects but should also aim towards creating a concern for the society with a view to finding positive solution to the problems faced by the people. We need to create the such passion among our self channel our vibrate energy.

Creativity has got multiple dimension like invention, innovation, discoveries. It can imagine or invent something new by coming, changing, or replying exiting ideas. Creativity has an attitude to accept change and newness, a willingness to play with ideas and possibilities, flexibility of outlook, the habit of enjoying the good, while looking for ways to improve it. Creativity has a process to work hard and to improve ideas and solutions continuously by making gradual alterations and refinements to their works. So question is what is right time for creativity, of course it student's life. The important aspect of creativity is seeing the same things as everybody else but thinking different. Imagination generates creativity, creativity leads to thinking. There is a need to nurture innovation at workplaces. Innovation is market driven. Innovation can also be in the form of improving performance of the product/system technique by adopting a change using alternative technologies. It is the thorough process of innovation that knowledge is converted into wealth and social good.

## Unique you

The aim of one's life should be to reach his full potential in body, mind, and heart and sprit.

When we see the light of electric bulb, our thought goes to the great inventor Thomas Alva Edison for his unique contribution towards the invention of electric

bulb and the electric lighting system. When we hear the sound of an aeroplane going over house we think of wright brothers, who proved it at a heavy risk and on their cost, that man could fly. The telephone ring reminds us the Alexander Graham Bell. When everybody see travel as an experience or a voyage, a unique person, during his see travel from United Kingdom to India, was pondering why the horizon where the sky and see meet looks blue. His research resulted in explaining the phenomena of scattering of light -this unique scientist Sir CV Raman was awarded Noble Prize. The word is fortunate to have a great leader of 20th century, father of the nation, Mahatma Gandhi, who helped India to get its freedom, and also paved the way of South Africa movement against apartheid. One woman scientist got two Noble Prizes; first in 1903 and second in 1911. One was for discovering radium, and the other was for her pioneering research in chemistry. She is discoverer of radiation that saved and saving thousands and thousands of lives of cancer patients. And also now by irradiating the seeds certain types of agriculture crops are giving very high yields. The same radiation phenomenon is used both for power generation and also nuclear weapon system. Who is the great lady in material world and healthcare world? The scientist is Madam Marie Curie.

*We remember the unique participation of Henry Ford as on the vehicle running on the road.* And in India we can't forget the unique contribution of the missile man DR. APJ Abdul Kalam. *All of mention above and rest of other than had the unique talent and they have strong desire to help the society. They were the unique. If you don't know your unique talent you should read the biography of most successful people. You should try to meet the topper of the particular field. Anybody came on earth have special unique latent but it is needed to find within you.*

Now the question is, Are you willing to become a unique personality? I have, so far, I teach and train and meet thousands of the youth in all over India in urban as well as in rural. Every youth want to be unique like you as reader of the book. And the world all around you is doing its best to make you unique.

The challenge is to fight the hardest battle, which any human being can ever imagine; and never stop fighting until you arrive at your destined place that is a, unique you. You have to decide, do you want to unique or everybody else.

*As said above everyone is unique but we have battle to be unique. There are five tools for building a unique personality:*

- *You must have the aim in the life.*

- *You must continuously acquire the knowledge.*

- *You must work hard.*

- *You must preserve to defeat the problems.*

- *You must have a strong desire to be success.*

*These are the proven steps, if you acquire these five qualities, then you can achieve whatever your vision.*

*"Don't keep forever on the public road, going only where others have gone. Leave the beaten track occasionally and dive into the woods. You will be certain to find something you have never seen before. It will be a little thing but don't ignore it. Follow it up, Explore all around it, one discovery will lead to another, and before you know it, you will have something worth thinking about".*

# Four

## Discipline

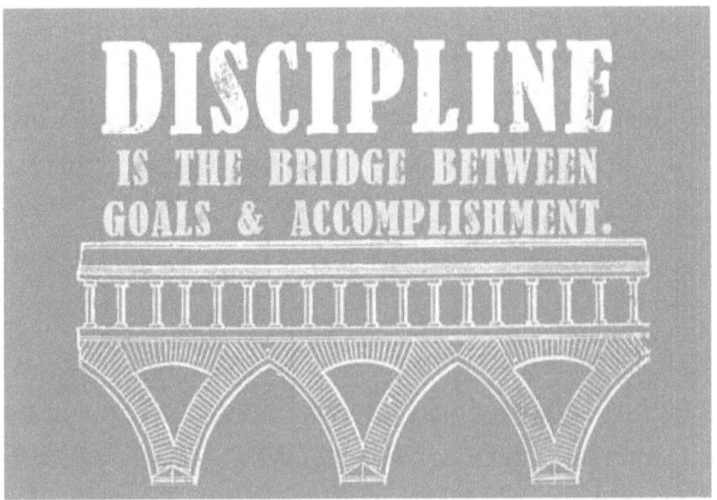


Success is nothing more than a few simple disciplined practical's every day. Any country or a society or an individual will not succeed, if he is not disciplined. Similarly, if the army and the police refuse to carry out the orders of their Generals and Commanders, the enemy and hooligans will have no difficulty in establishing their sway in the country.

In this way, if the students are not disciplined they will learn nothing and the purpose of education will be defeated.

To maintain goals in your life it is very important to stay disciplined. It helps the students to stay motivated. Good discipline is essential for the student to complete all their assignment works.

Discipline in school or collage life is very important tool. We can not be well educated without discipline. Discipline is a set of rules and regulations that reminds us the proper code of behavior.

Most successful people are expert in discipline on a daily basis. Discipline brings stability and structure into a person's life.

*"Discipline is doing what needs to be done*
*even though you don't want to"*

Discipline means order or code of behavior. The purpose of discipline is correct behavior. It is not designed to punish or embarrass anyone. Discipline is a positive method of teaching a child self confidence and responsibility. Punishment is quite different from discipline. Punishment may be physical as in spanking hitting of causing pain. But discipline is refining fire by which the talent become ability. Discipline is the key of development. If you have to keep yourself in discipline by others it feels very uncomfortable. So we have to be self-disciplined.

Self-discipline refreshes the ability to control one's own feelings. Self-discipline feeds to overcome one's own weakness. Life without self-discipline is no life. He need to guided by rules. We have to be respectful to our elders, parents and teachers. We must obey seniors.

## Self-discipline (Importance)

Self-discipline is must needed for success in life. Discipline is a must whatever we are at school / collage play ground or at home. It is equally necessary whatever we are in the school / collage or on playground. Our life, our society, our country or even the world will go astray without discipline. So some sort discipline is required every where.

Self-discipline has to be mandatory at every walk of life. Childhood or student's life is the best period to learn discipline. The young mind learns things quickly and easily. At school, the students are taught to behalf well. Even on playground the students are taught to follow the rules of the games. So the student's days are the most formative period in which the value of self-discipline can be learnt easily and fast.

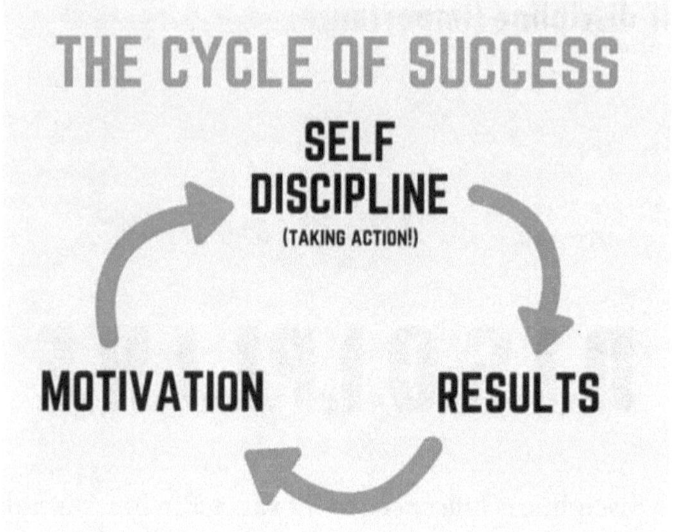


Without self-discipline a man is like an animal. His life and actions become animal's life. In present days the self-discipline is a great form of life. It is growing in the every walk of life. Discipline is necessary in all spheres of life.

In personal life too, one has to practice dip line for a stable and worthy life. In fact life is best enjoyed only if discipline is maintained Nothing can't be properly enjoyed, not even a game of cricket or a musical concert, if indiscipline is allowed to invade it. We should all try to maintain discipline in our lives.

Our future life will start from our student's life. In student life, we would be founded our future life. The works in the time of student life will decide our future, what would we make out of it.

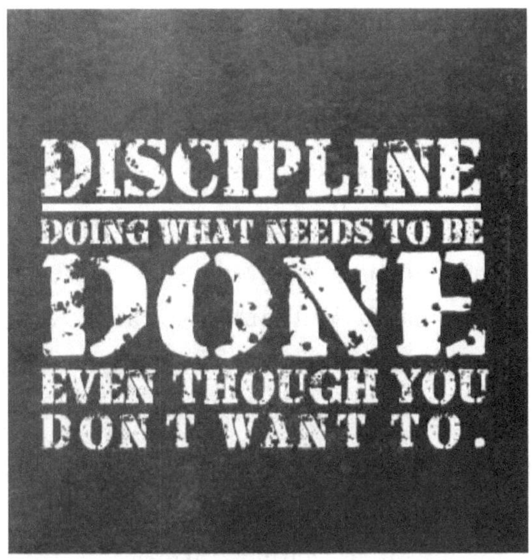


*"we can live the life by chance or*
*we can live life by choice"*

In fact, self-discipline is a good thing. It builds character of individual's. It develops strength and identity. It creates a sense of co-operation. So self-discipline must be taught from the very childhood. It is a key to success. Higher is the sense of discipline better to himself society and world. Discipline creates a sense of co-operation.

Self-discipline is no doubt an incredible mechanism that we can use to propel us forward toward our goals. If used correctly, it can dramatically expedite our results and accelerate productivity. However, when used unproductively, it can very quickly lead us down the rabbit hole of perfectionism and stagnation. It just depends on how you choose to use it.

Ultimately, **self-discipline isn't really that difficult to nurture. All you need is a little inspiration to kick in.**

With inspiration, self-discipline becomes somewhat of an after thought. Because when we're feeling inspired that surge of energy naturally drives us forward.

When we're feeling inspired, we're more committed to the task at hand. Without inspiration though, our commitment levels tend to waver, and it subsequently makes it more challenging to exercise self-discipline.

Given this, it's critical that you keep your commitment alive by looking for inspiration in everything you do. You can, for instance, gather inspiration from books, from people, from quotes, from movies, from current events, from magazines, through a vision poster, through journaling your learning experiences, etc. You can even find inspiration through stories of how other people achieved their goals.

In the end, though, inspiration without action leads to nothing. You must use inspiration as a platform to help you take massive and proactive action in the direction of your objectives. Only in this way will your self-discipline grow and thrive as you strive to achieve your goals.

> *"Excellence is a journey, Discipline is the vehicle"*

## You are what your habits are

In all walks of human life, the habits relating to the formation of thoughts, emotions and action play an important role. There are habit which mould personality or harm it.

If we continually do something, good or bad, for a sufficiently long time it influences our mind and our nervous system so strongly that the habit becomes a part of our nature and is carried out like our involuntary actions.

A retired soldier was walking on the road, carrying a load of grocery on his head. A mischievous boy had seen him walk on the road several times. One day when the solider was walking absent-minded along the road by the side of ditch, he shouted aloud; Attention !. The moment the retired solider heard the word 'attention', he dropped his arm, which were until then supporting a bundle, stood erect and was about to offer salute. The bundle on his head fell into ditch and the things within were scattered helter-skelter. Before he became aware of the mischief, the incident had taken place. As he had long been subjected to military exercise, his mind acted mechanically and spontaneously at a mere suggestion !.

Many are not aware of the tremendous controlling power of habits. It is habit that acts obstructions to us escaping from complicated or embarrassing situation. Every day, without own knowledge, we try to adapt to our place and environment. Observe those who have the habit of smoking a cigarette after breakfast. Suppose there is no stock of cigarette in their pocket, they don't mind even walking two miles to a shop to buy a cigarette. Of course, we need not mean only bad habits when refer to habits.

All kinds of habits control the individual and mould his personality with their powerful influence. Our achievement, ideas, contradictions, tastes, and acquisitions, love, and, hate, anger and anxiety, secrete, and deceits, pride, and self-esteem, inclinations, and tendencies – all these are the habits that we have gathered from our surrounding, consciously or unconsciously. There is an adage in English about the difficulty of feeling oneself from an ingrained habit. Even if you remove the first letter 'h' from it a bit remains. If the letter 'a' is removed 'bit' remains. If 'b' is removed it remains. Do you now realize how strong the effect of habit is !.

## Forming a good habit

In order to form a good habit and retain it firmly in one's physical and mental make-up, one should begins with a firm determination.

Instability and indecision mark the state of mind which is not subject to any discipline. The energies of an undisciplined mind are scattered in many directions and are wasted. A person with an unsteady mind can not achieve anything worthwhile. By doing all works, big or small, with concentration and mathematically, one gathers the ability to work efficiency and ease.

Look at a skilled cyclist. He is able to speak to his/ her friends, enjoy the beauty of the scenery around him, negotiate between the vehicles and people moving on the road, and ride on without any anxiety, confusion or fear. When he has to apply the brakes he does so, almost involuntarily.

As he has cultivate the habit, he don't have to spend so much of his energy, as he would have needed if he didn't have practice. It is easy to cultivate a second constructive habit, if one habit is firmly rooted in one's scheme of things. For instance, while bathing one could commit to memory of mathematical formula, a passage of poetry or a verse. While the activity of taking a bath goes on uninterrupted, acquisition of knowledge or a skill will also have take place.

We should be alert to utilize every opportunity which can induce us to take up continuous practice for the sake of useful skill. We should be careful to create situation in terms of place and time which will effectively resist the temptations that might drag us into the former rut of recklessness or indecision. In short, every opportunity should be used to safeguard your resolution or determination to do your utmost to enhance your quality as a person. Only then can you overcome temptations that may lead you to break your own resolve.

The practice that you have started should not be given up, even for a day, until the new habit has become a part of your mental and nervous system. If you skip the practice even for a day for some reason, the next day your mind invents some excuse for postponing it further.

## Importance of discipline

Any attempt to develop will-power shall fail unless we develop discipline along with it. Every student knows what he or she must do to pass the exams. Yet only those who have the habit of setting aside a few hours everyday to study and revise their lessons can make any progress. Students who lack this discipline may be very brilliant, but they will still not fare well in the exams.

Trying to improve life through various methods, but completely ignoring the essential point discipline, serves no purpose. Getting up at whatever time one likes, skipping breakfast, having lunch at 1pm on one day and 3pm on another, such pattern of behavior is indicative of indiscipline and irregularity. Such a mind will be unfocused and unable to achieve anything.

Discipline is a concept everyone is aware of, but few truly understand. The most successful people in life exert discipline on a daily basis. It is vital to every living being and without it, the world around us would be chaos.

To be a great and inspiring leader, you must constantly display restraint. Not giving into something you truly want is a sign of strength. Making the right decisions in life can make or break you, and this type of person tends to make the right decisions. Regardless of where you exert this self-restraint, it will help to promote achievement in your life.

"Talent without discipline is like an octopus on roller skates. There's plenty of movement, but you never know if it's going to be forward, backwards, or sideways."

Discipline brings stability and structure into a person's life. It teaches a person to be responsible and respectful. The observance of well-defined rules is the basis of society. If there is no discipline, people would do whatever they want and make mistakes without putting the consideration of others first and foremost. It promotes good human behavior to better society and make it a more enjoyable place for everyone to live.

The ability for an individual to have self-restraint allows them to behave in a consistently stringent and controlled manner. Lack of this ability can have disastrous results. Do you think a company is going to tolerate a person who is consistently late to work or who procrastinates in doing their work? It is evident how these behaviours will weaken the image of a business.

> *"Mental toughness is many things and rather difficult*
> *to explain. Its qualities are sacrifice and self-denial.*
> *Also, most importantly, it is combined with a perfectly*
> *disciplined will that refuses to give in. It's a state of mind*
> *-- you could call it character in action."*
>
> *—Vince Lombardi*

Think about athletics; discipline is the fundamental aspect on which sports have been created. Every player must adhere to the rules of the game. This is why umpires and referees exist. Whoever does not follow these guidelines will be penalized for violating the rules of the sport.

Persons in high authority must demonstrate high levels of restraint constantly; they cannot just speak however they see fit. A smart leader knows when to hold his tongue and when to speak. Discipline helps to train a person's mind and character, building a sense of self-control and the practice of obedience.

"Self-discipline is a form of freedom. Freedom from laziness and lethargy, freedom from the expectations and demands of others, freedom from weakness and fear — and doubt. Self-discipline allows a pitcher to feel his individuality, his inner strength, his talent. He is master of, rather than a slave to, his thoughts and emotions."

There are two types of discipline: internal and external. Internal discipline is your self-restraint and your ability to differentiate right from wrong. External discipline is according to societal norms, such as following the law. It is not sufficient enough to possess great qualities; we need the ability to manage them.

Too many people are susceptible to instant gratification. People lacking control are unable to look at the long-term effects of their actions. This further demonstrates why this is such a crucial skill to have in life. It is probably the most crucial factor when trying to achieve a goal. It allows you to choose from different options and by following these options you can garner the success you sought out for. It additionally gives you the authority to overcome any obstacles that come your way.

"Discipline is the bridge between goals and accomplishment."

This ability can be developed or strengthened at any given time if you put your mind to it. Make promises and make sure you deliver. Make the genuine effort to align your actions and behaviours with your thoughts. Exercise; get your mind and body into shape. Resist the urge to give into negative behaviours, instead focus on all of the positive attributes.

## Aim of life/Goal

Everybody should have the aim of life. Aimless life is nothing. Aimless life is like a kite without string. It will go where ever the wind will take it. So in the case of student must have the goal. It may be small goal or a big goal. To activate the talent or abilities in yourself you should have a goal in your life. The goal need not be just the desire salvation. There should be a specific and clear goal in everybody's life. Of course, a momentary desire is not a goal. And it is not enough to have a desire to succeed on the task you have set for yourself. It is necessary to act in the proper manner so that it is carried out in the prescribed time. Unless you have a working plan, your valuable mental energy and time will be wasted.

You may have thought of giving a speech before an audience, planned to run a business or become an artist or writer. You may just wish to improve your performance in your education and get more. Whatever it may be, you have to have a clear idea about your goal or aim. It is that desire or idea that induced the spirit to translate the idea into action.

To be able to overcome uncertainty and vacillation, you have to ask yourself what it is that you most desire for yourself. Then it becomes clear to you what it is that you most desire for yourself. Then it becomes clear to you what main goal you should have for yourself in your life. Then your mind devotes its energy to fulfilment of desire.

## Importance of Aim in Life

*"A soul without a high aim is like a ship without a rudder."*

**—Eileen Caddy**

The rudder of a ship steers the ship to a particular destination. Similarly aim or goal set by us directs our life to a particular destination. A life without an aim is absolutely meaningless. Thus, needless to say that in order to shape up one's life, one must not only have a proper aim in life but should also have a profound desire to achieve it.

Aim can also be termed as Goal or Target. Once the goal is set, human minds start formulating several ways and means following which the target set can be reached. All our thoughts and efforts are channelized in that specific direction leading towards the target. Many a times we find the route to the target is very tough and turbulent. There are various obstacles overcoming which becomes quite a difficult task for us, we feel completely exhausted, thereby losing our focus, self-confidence, concentration and most importantly our hope. Precisely speaking it is the challenge that life throws at us, our destiny starts testing our patience, confidence, courage and stamina. At this stage, we should not feel despaired, instead we should scrutinize every step of our movement, learning from our previous mistakes. This is the time when our intense desire of achieving our aim replenishes us with self-confidence, optimism, stamina and enthusiasm which helps to regain our positive energy to fight back and throwing a challenge towards life, destiny in return.

In other words we can say that our intense desire to achieve our goal rejuvenates our minds in all possible ways, we regain our stamina, energy, enthusiasm to experiment with our potential, our capabilities, our expertise. Thus we can say that setting an aim in life and being passionate enough to achieve it do not only direct our life to a particular destination but also sharpen and strengthen our mind and body, thereby firming our character in totality.

In life we all set our goals and pursue them to the best of our capacity, but all our goals need not be money oriented. Certain goals are set to serve humanity. Sometimes certain goal set by human beings are so noble that momentary factor turns out to be very insignificant compared to the chastity of such an aim. For instance, Mother Teresa, her sole aim in life was to serve the downtrodden and distressed people surviving in this world. The world salutes Mother Teresa for her gracious contribution to the society.

Unfortunately, today we all are accustomed to materialistic life to such an extent that all our aims are mostly money-oriented in nature. In order to live a healthy life and to maintain a proper standard of living we do require money. Money is essential for survival, but let us not forget we are human beings and not machines. As human beings we do have moral responsibilities towards our families, society, country, but our extremely money-oriented ambitions are making us mercenary, exterminating our humane qualities in totality, thereby giving birth to several malicious qualities in human minds. This is one reason why today a certain category of people do not hesitate to dump their old, ailing, helpless parents in old age homes.

Human beings are blessed with several benevolent instincts, to name a few - love, compassion, respect, generosity, most importantly - unique mind power which can distinguish between the right and the wrong. Therefore we should exercise our mind power to such a level that our mind should guide us to take only righteous steps and decisions in life. Humans without benevolent instincts, a thoughtful compassionate mind is same as a brutal animal. We should always maintain a balance between our ambition and our moral responsibilities, our inefficiency in striking a proper balance between the two is giving birth to several family, social problems which is rottening the society.

It is very important to have a constructive aim in life. Our aims should construct our lives with everything virtuous, righteous that life has to offer in plenty. We should always remember that for purchasing the best quality product from the market we have to pay a high price. Similarly higher our aim, tougher will be the road leading to the target, but with complete focus, concentration, dedication we can reach our goal, breaking all barriers and obstacles. An aim which is destructive in nature might provide us with all luxuries but it robs us of all humane qualities.

## Find your weakness

We all have weaknesses. Whether they're snacks such as potato chips or chocolate chip cookies, or technology such as Facebook or the latest addictive game app, they have similar effects on us.

Acknowledge your shortcomings, whatever they may be. Too often people either try to pretend their vulnerabilities don't exist or cover up any pitfalls in their lives. Own up to your flaws. You can't overcome them until you do

## Remove temptations

Like the saying goes, "out of sight, out of mind." It may seem silly, but this phrase offers powerful advice. By simply removing your biggest temptations from your environment, you will greatly improve your self-discipline.

If you want to eat healthier, don't buy junk food. If you want to improve your productivity at work, turn off notifications and silent your cell phone. The fewer distractions you have, the more focused you will be on accomplishing your goals. Set yourself up for success by ditching bad influences.

## Plan and action

If you hope to achieve self-discipline, you must have a clear vision of what you hope to accomplish. You must also have an understanding of what success means to you. After all, if you don't know where you are going, it's easy to lose your way or get side tracked.

A clear plan outlines each step you must take in order to reach your goals. Figure out who you are and what you are about. Create a mantra to keep yourself focused. Successful people use this technique to stay on track and establish a clear finish line.

## Build your self-confidence

We aren't born with self-discipline -- it's a learned behaviour. And just like any other skill you want to master, it requires daily practice and repetition. Just like going to the gym, willpower and self-discipline take a lot of work. The effort and focus that self-discipline requires can be draining.

As time passes, it can become more and more difficult to keep your willpower in check. The bigger the temptation or decision, the more challenging it can feel to tackle other tasks that also require self-control. So work on building your self-discipline through daily diligence.

## Adopt new simple good habits

Acquiring self-discipline and working to install a new habit can feel daunting at first, especially if you focus on the entire task at hand. To avoid feeling intimidated, keep it simple. Break your goal into small, double steps. Instead of trying to change everything at once, focus on doing one thing consistently and master self-discipline with that goal in mind.

If you're trying to get in shape, start by working out 10 or 15 minutes a day. If you're trying to achieve better sleep habits, start by going to bed 15 minutes earlier each night. If you want to eat healthier, start by prepping lunch the night before to take with you in the morning. Take baby steps. Eventually, when you're ready, you can add more goals to your list.

## Take healthy diet

The feeling of being hungry -that angry, annoyed, irritated sensation you get when you're hungry; is real and can have a substantial impact on willpower. Research has proven that low blood sugar often weakens a person's resolve, making you grumpy and pessimistic.

When you're hungry, your ability to concentrate suffers and your brain doesn't function as well. Your self-control is likely weakened in all areas, including diet, exercise, work and relationships. So fuel up with healthy snacks and regular meals to keep yourself in check.

## Change your perception about will power

According to a study by Stanford University, the amount of willpower a person has is determined by his beliefs. If you believe you have a limited amount of willpower, you probably won't surpass those limits. If you don't place a limit on your self-control, you are less likely to exhaust yourself before meeting your goals.

In short, it may be that our internal conceptions about willpower and self-control determine how much of them we have. If you can remove these subconscious obstacles and truly believe you can do it, then you will give yourself an extra boost of motivation toward making those goals a reality.

## Always keep backup plan

Psychologists use a technique to boost willpower called "implementation intention." That's when you give yourself a plan to deal with a potentially difficult situation you know you will likely face. For instance, imagine that you're working on eating healthier, but you're on your way to a party where food will be served.

Before you go, tell yourself that instead of diving into a plate of cheese and crackers, you will sip a glass of water and focus on mingling. Going in with a plan will help give you the mindset and the self-control necessary for the situation. You will also save energy by not having to make a sudden decision based on your emotional state.

## Reward or appreciate yourself

Give yourself something to be excited about by planning a reward when you accomplish your goals. Just like when you were a little kid and got a treat for good behaviour, having something to look forward to gives you the motivation to succeed.

Anticipation is powerful. It gives you something to obsess over and focus on, so you're not only thinking of what you are trying to change. And when you achieve your goal, find a new goal and a new reward to keep yourself moving forward.

## Forgive yourself and move forward

Even with all of our best intentions and well-laid plans, we sometimes fall short. It happens. You will have ups and downs, great successes and dismal failures. The key is to keep moving forward.

If you stumble, acknowledge what caused it and move on. Don't let yourself get wrapped up in guilt, anger or frustration, because these emotions will only drag you further down and impede future progress. Learn from your missteps and forgive yourself. Then get your head back in the game and refocus on your goals.

# Five

## Energetic or Motivated

Student should be energetic in each field of life. If any of us is not energetic or lazy we may loose many of the opportunities. Main working field of the student are school/collage, playground, coaching center and home also. Student keep himself always ready to learn in each field of life. *Be energetic means to be motivated.* If life is vehicle then motivation is the driving force which the vehicle. Motivation plays a vital role in everyone's life. Motivation is the energy to success. It is something which drives you. Actually it is a force that keeps you going, keep you energized while you pursue your dreams. Many students face the problem of lack of motivation. Students begin their study but slowly get less motivated or not so energetic with books or at any task.

As a student it is important for you to stay motivated for your goal but if you are not, means you are not serious or may be you have not a sufficient reason. Without purpose it very difficult to be motivated or energetic.

So, student should make the some aim of life. What you want to become in your future life, these are the essential to be motivated or always be energetic. The burning desire be to success in the life or live your dream life, it is compulsory to be motivated and energetic. Without motivation, nobody fulfill its dream. Our mind is designed in such way that it is driven by purpose.

When your mind is clear about what and why you want to do something. It is not just important to have a goal to achieve but it is equally important to answer the question -why do you want to achieve that goal ?.Your mind and heart should be clear about why you want to achieve that goal. So student be energetic and be motivated.

## Importance of Thoughts

It is clear as daylight that thoughts and emotions, are the two most important influences upon man's life. Who want to walk on the path of progress should understand the great power of thought. Whenever a thought associated with self confidence and optimism leads to an action, it generally a constructive result. Whenever a thought associated with fear and doubts leads to an action, it produce generally a negative result. Regarding the power of mind there is an incontrovertible law; ' like attracts like, like begets like, like becomes like'.

In other words, when we think good thoughts, they lead us to good people and good things in life. When we think evil thoughts they led us to evil people and evil things in life.

This truth reaffirmed by modern experimental research, was started by Gautam buddha about two thousand and five hundred years ago...

*"What we are today, is the fruit of our thoughts. Thoughts are the bases of our current situation. It is made up of our thoughts. If a man speaks, having good thoughts in his mind, and acts according, happiness follows him as shadow follows man. If another man goes on thinking evil thoughts and acts accordingly grief pursues him, just as wheels follow the legs of the horses drawing a carriage".*

These profound statements of the Great One contain an eternal truth and reflect the great importance of the thoughts.

We may have large mammals so far in innumerable debilitating, humiliating thoughts. Should we proceed on the path of progress, we should, right from now on, absorb good thoughts, one by one, and raise our life. If our body is smeared with dirt, no screaming can clean us. We have to wash our-self with clean water. We should cultivate good thoughts and preserve good thoughts. Then, evil thoughts can gradually abandon us. It would be greatly helpful to reflect on the message of the life of great man who have been free from all kinds of egotism and who have been seekers of truth. So you should be energetic with positive and creative thoughts.

## Thoughts gives energy

The following are the few ideas about the true nature of thoughts; once a thought arises in your mind, there is every likelihood that it will occur in the mind. If a thought repeats five, ten, or twenty times, it becomes an integral part of mind. Though we may not deliberating try to recall it, it is dormant in the depth in the mind. The powerful thought in your mind exerts its influence not only on yourself but also on those who are near you. If you think well of others, they will also wish you well.

## Role Of Motivation In Student Life

Motivation states that, it is a drive that encourage actions or feeling. To motivate means to encourage and inspire. motivation can also means igniting the spark for action. "motivation arouses interest. interest is the mother of attention and attention is the mother of learning. Thus to secure learning you must first catch the mother, grandmother and great grandmother. Motivation is the indispensable technique for learning.it energies and accelerates the behaviour of learner. Desirable changes in learner's behaviour are only possible when the learner is properly motivated. Thus we can say that no learning is possible without motivation.

## Type of Motivation

1. External Motivation (Extrinsic Motivation).

2. Internal Motivation (Intrinsic Motivation).

1. External Motivation:-External motivation comes from outside. Examples of external motivation is money, societal approval, fame or fear.

2. Internal Motivation:-Internal motivation comes within,pride,a sense of achievement, responsibility and beliefs. Internal motivation is the inner gratification, not for success or winning.

## Common Factors of Motivation

Following factors plays very important role to motivated either internal and external motivation are:

### Incentive

Internal motivation can also take the form of incentives. An incentive is something the student perceives as having the capability of satisfying an aroused motive. It drive the student to action aimed at acquiring the incentive like grades, praise, award, any certification etc.. The student motivated by curiosity has understanding or knowledge as his or her incentive. If the achievement is the motive, then success, honour or good grades will serve as incentives.

### Recognition

Recognition is the important external motivator. Recognition means being appreciated, being treated with respect and dignity, and feeling a sense of belonging. Recognition is external because it originates from outside, but its feelings are internal

## Responsibility

It gives a person a feeling belonging and ownership. He/she becomes the part of big picture if we give them responsibility. Actually lack of responsibility is demotivating factor. Responsibility is internal as it originates from within.

## Attitude

Attitude means an outlook and a tendency readiness to respond in favourable or unfavourable manner to particular people, object, concept, or situations. Attitude carry a strong emotional component. and therefore can never be natural. Attitude is important determiners of behaviour. Both interest and attitude are learned behaviour, in that they are not inherited or genetically endowed.

## Aspiration

A student's aspiration or motive is his hope or longing for a certain kind of achievement. With a certain level of aspiration, the student will try; without it. He will make little or no effort.

## Fear

*Another force that motivates is fear. Fear of failure is the one type of motivation. We fear criticism, if you terrified with a negative result, you run harder towards the opposite direction.*

## Money

Money also gives us motivation. Most of time money drive human being. Money has a power to enjoy the life. Actually it is what from that we buy the fun, entertainment, and enjoy the life. Money have an intrinsic power from that we fulfil in our daily requirements. The desire to have more money act as a force that keeps you working towards your aim.

## Success

To be success is the main source of motivation. The desire of the success is the root cause of the motivation or to be energetic. Motivation either internal or external itself energies you to do the best. Highest rate of motivation is the highest chance of success.

## Need

It refers to lack of something, biological, or psychological in a man. A student who comes to know or realize that he lacks something and that he needs it, is likely to strive for attending it, for examples, need for achievement, need for recognition. need for affiliation, need for dominance and more like. Whatever the motivates be, study suggests people who feel a need for achievement are usually oriented towards the future and set long term goals. From many case study and different survey it is seen that most successful people in the world are comes from poor and needy families. So needs are the most powerful source of motivation. So the teacher and parents must be careful to help them to set their realistic goal and help them to identify their potential, needs, interest and weakness also and moreover then endeavour to fulfil their needs.

## Steps to be Energetic or Motivated

People who are fun loving and energetic tend to live a healthier lifestyle. When your feelings about yourself are improved, you have the ability to cope with stress and enjoy life more. If you feel you could be more fun loving and energetic, you can bring these sides up in various ways.

### *Engage in regular exercise*

Exercise helps improve your overall health, makes you stronger, and makes your body work more efficiently. All these combined will make you more energetic.

- Choose exercise activities that you enjoy. Some people associate exercising with going to the gym or physical education class, but that is only a small fraction of what exercise can be. You can go walking, hiking, dancing, bicycling, or jogging, or you can play tennis, golf, racquetball, or some other sport.

- Not only will exercise improve your health and make you feel more energetic, it also helps you to become happier, more positive, and less anxious.

- Engage in some form of physical exercise at least 3-4 times or 150 minutes per week.

### Take healthy diet

Our bodies need fuel for energy; that fuel is food. Build your diet around healthy non-processed foods that provide all the necessary nutrients and help raise your energy levels.

- Avoid foods high in sugar and low in nutrition (called empty-calorie foods), such as pre-packaged meals, chips, sodas, and candy bars. These foods actually decrease energy levels after providing a very short energy boost.

- An ideal mix of ingredients to eat includes foods that provide complex carbohydrates, are low in fat, and contain moderate amount of protein.

- Spread your daily calories evenly and avoid skipping a meal only to have a huge meal later. If possible, eat five meals a day, keeping the amount of calories in a day where you want.

- Do not skip any meals. This will cause a loss of energy. Your body needs food to keep going in the same way a vehicle needs gas to keep going.

- Also, drink plenty of water. Dehydration leads to low energy. Drink 8-9 glasses of water each day.

### Ensure you get healthy meal

B vitamins and iron are important micronutrients that help support your energy levels. If you are deficient in these nutrients, you can experience lowered energy levels.

- B vitamins and iron are extremely important for your body's ability to create and use energy. Vitamin 12, vitamin 6, thiamine, niacin, and folic acid support your body's energy metabolism, while iron is needed for healthy red blood cells that are responsible for carrying oxygen.

- Deficiency in B vitamins and iron can lead to anaemia and fatigue.

- If you are not getting enough of these and other micronutrients in your diet, consider taking a multivitamin with iron and essential B vitamins.

### Get enough sleep.

If you suffer from lack of energy, it might be because you are not getting enough sleep. According to the Sleep Foundation, adults should get between 7 and 9 hours of sleep each night.

- Make sure you get enough sleep. Set a regular bedtime and stick to it every night, even during the weekends. If you need to adjust your bedtime, make small daily increments (15 min earlier every night) until you achieve the target bedtime. Also, wake up the same time every morning.

- Avoid heavy meals and too much just before bedtime as these might make sleeping more difficult.

- If you suffer from insomnia or sleep disturbances, it can lead to fatigue and lack of motivation. However, fatigue can also be a sign of a more serious health condition. If you don't get energized by getting enough sleep and good nutrition, you should get evaluated by your doctor.

### Practice yoga

Practicing yoga can help reduce fatigue and boost your energy levels in addition to the other health benefits it has to your muscles and cardiovascular system.

During yoga poses, breathe deeply to bring fresh oxygen to your blood. This will stimulate your nervous system and make you feel more energetic.

Try the following breathing exercise; sit on the floor with your spine straight. Breathe in through your nose and count to four. Then exhale while counting to eight. Repeat.

- Try the *Uttanasana* yoga pose, which is an energizing forward bend; start by standing and bending forward and down. Keep your knees slightly bent and allow your upper body to hang toward the toes. Breathe deeply, while allowing your spine to lengthen.

### Control your stress

Stress can be a debilitating condition associated with emotional and physical tension, and anxiety. In order to bring your fun-loving side up, try to reduce or eliminate stress in your life.

- Stress can result from both the negative (such as trouble at work or school) and positive (planning a friend's birthday party) events in your life.

- Nobody is a stranger to stress; however, if you experience stress long-term, it can negatively impact your health.

Take steps to control stress and allow yourself to be more fun loving. Stress can be controlled by exercising regularly, resting and relaxing enough, eating a healthy diet, and treating yourself to something special.

### Deal with sadness

Like stress, sadness or feeling blue can also affect your emotional and physical well being and dampen your fun-loving side.

If you are sad, you may also suffer from low enthusiasm, lethargy, and/or low self-esteem. If you are feeling low in energy, drive, and hope, it is more challenging to be fun-loving.

Sometimes beating sadness can be as easy as leaving the house and diverting your sadness to something positive and fun.

When you are feeling blue you might keep yourself isolated and avoid spending time with others. If you find yourself spending all your time alone at home, force yourself out of the house.

You can go shopping, walking, or catch a funny movie at the theater. Anything that gets you out of the house and spend time with your friends and family will do.

The hardest step is to leave the house, but once you do it and are out, you can often find yourself forgetting the sadness and enjoying life.

If you cannot beat your sadness, consider seeking medical attention to determine if you may suffer from depression. Your doctor can prescribe antidepressants to treat depression.

Seasonal depression is a common condition; an estimated 6.7% of U.S. population suffered from at least one depressive episode in 2013.

Caution: serious, untreated depression can lead to suicidal thoughts. If you or someone you know suffer from depression or a depressive episode, seek help immediately.

### Find an activity that makes you happy

If you feel that you are not fun-loving because you never do anything that is fun, then the only way to fix that is to find an activity that makes you happy and excited.

The activity that makes you happy can differ tremendously depending what type of person you are. Extroverts can find their happiness by seeking crowds and being in the centre of attention, while introverts may find their energy in solitude. Whatever the activity, you need to figure it out yourself and then just do it.

If you love the outdoors and enjoy the nature, go hiking, skiing, running, swimming, or bicycling. These are easy-to-do activities that require little planning and equipment and you can easily do by yourself.

Or try something new and go horseback riding, rock climbing, parasailing, backpacking, etc. You may surprise yourself and find an inner happiness you never knew existed.

If you are the type that requires company and/or encouragement to try new things, ask your friend to come along. Finding a new hobby to do together can be a great way to bring your fun-loving side up too.

## Learn to think more positively

Negative thoughts and feelings have the capability to bring you down and lower your self-esteem. Learning to see the positive side in life can have a transforming effect and allow you to release your fun-loving side.

- You may not always be able to control your external environment, but you can control your inner thoughts. Even in tough situations, thinking positively can help you overcome barriers and release your fun-loving side.

- Seek situations that bring out the best in you and then learn to transfer that feeling to situations that might not bring out the best in you. This way you can learn to think positively even in situations that might normally bring out negative thoughts.

- Focus on what is good in your life and write it down on a paper. Then carry that paper with you. When you find yourself down or unhappy, read through that list and try to change your negative thoughts to positive thoughts (e.g., the glass is half full, not half empty).

- You can also break free from negative thoughts by telling yourself "I can" and not allowing disrespectful people or bad situations bring you down.

## Honour and respect yourself

Being able to be more fun-loving means you need to honour and love yourself first. Honouring yourself means to honour your life and what you have accomplished and created. This includes friendships, family, children, and even strangers that you have connected with.

- In order to honour yourself, you need to accept yourself for who you are. Only when you understand who you are and can embrace that person, can you bring your fun-loving side up.

- To learn to honour yourself, list your biggest achievements on a paper (e.g., graduated from school, had children, bought a house, climbed a mountain, achieved a personal goal, etc). Then, focus on those achievements and allow yourself to gain respect for yourself through them.

## Break out of your comfort zone

Sometimes being more fun loving means you need to allow yourself to try new things instead of only doing things you have become comfortable or accustomed with.

- Often we keep ourselves contained in a zone where we are comfortable, but that does not mean that is the place where we are happiest.

- Allow yourself to try new things, take chances, and have fun. However, there are limitations to what you can and what you should do and you should never try or do things that cause harm to you or others.

- To break out, first understand your comfort zone and how you tend to stay in it naturally. Once you understand your comfort zone, change your normal way of thinking and acting and slowly break out of it.

For example, start by making a list of all the things that you do to avoid uncertainty (e.g., are there situations that you avoid, do you check on your kids constantly, do you suffer from lack of trust).

Once you have your list, start by picking the small items that you can do to break out of the cycle (e.g., go to a place you have never visited before, seek situations you normally avoid, allow yourself to be more trusting).

- Keep a record of all the times you succeeded in your goal and what happened (e.g., what happened when you visited a new place or pursued an unfamiliar situation).

# Six

## Never Lazy

A student must not be lazy. He should never be lazy at any stage of life i.e. school /collage, homework and playground etc. Laziness is a habit rather than a mental health issue. It may reflect a lack of self-confidence, lack of positive recognition by others or a lack of interest in the activities.

Laziness is a condition that a person is unable to do something, not because he or she has no ability to do it, but because of unwilling and psychologically unprepared. However, laziness should not be confused with tiredness, mental disorder or schizophrenia, although there are few similar character trait associated with each. Everybody at one time or another has experienced laziness in his or her life, though it might not be possible to notice that you are lazy since nobody want to be associated with laziness.

## Effects of laziness

Many people fail in their life not because they were unable to succeed but due to laziness. In fact, laziness is associated with poverty and all sort of evil. People have become so lazy to extend that they are unable to prepare their food. It is due to laziness that most fast foods restaurants are developing around the globe.

However, the effects can be clearly seen as the rate of obese people keep on growing every single day. Similarly, obese related deaths which were uncommon in ancient days are often report every single day. The big question is, what is the reason behind the growing rate of laziness? To understand the laziness read the famous story '*The farmer and the lazy lark bird*'. Once upon a time there was a rich old farmer who lived by the river side. By the river side was a lark bird that hated hunting for worms to eat. The old farmer always admired its beautiful feathers so much.

One morning the farmer went and gathered a box full of worms and went all the way to the market that was near his farm. As he was going through the forest to the market, the lark bird saw the farmer and was curious to know what he was carrying in the box. The bird asked the farmer, "What do you have in the box you are carrying?" The farmer said that he was carrying worms in the box. He did not know that the bird loved worms. The lark bird was so curious and still wanted to know where the farmer was taking the worms. "I am taking the worms to the market so that I can trade them for feathers," the farmer answered the bird.

The bird was so interested in the worms and flew next to the farmer to strike a deal with him. The other lark birds warned him against this deal but the lazy bird did not listen, he wanted the worms and he wanted them quick!

The bird asked the farmer, "why don't you give me that box of worms in exchange for a feather, instead of going to the market. "The farmer agreed and gave the box of worms to the bird. The greedy lark bird in return plucked a feather and give it to the farmer. The next day the same thing happened and the bird plucked another feather from its body. Because of its laziness, it continued to trade its feathers for the next weeks until it was left with none on its body. The lark bird could no longer fly and it became so ugly and weak from the cold which led to its death. The moral of this story is that laziness kill you. The lark bird though it would get its food easily without working. It did not know that in the long run it would need its feathers to fly. If it hunted for the worms, the bird would have lived longer.

## Causes of Laziness

Actually, most individuals are not intrinsically lazy, although they are viewed to be lazy, since they are doing nothing for their life or the welfare of the society. However, the case might be so different with majority since they have not yet found what they want to participate in or they are hindered from doing it by one factor or the other. For instance, some jobs require levels of specialization or demands high capital to begin, and therefore hinders the individuals from doing them. Technology is good for human life and played a very significant role in human development. On the other hand, technology is making people too lazy to do anything without help of the technology. Most people are unable even to do the simple calculations without the help of calculator, not that they are incapable but because they are unwilling and unprepared psychologically to handle it. In fact, with the look of think at the present, technology will make the future generations too lazy to do anything on their own.

Hopelessness and fear makes an Individual to have low self-esteem and feel uncomfortable with success. In fact most orphans and children from poor family background have the courage to face life with enthusiastic and therefore, they find laziness as means of sabotaging themselves.

Study is main duty of students. Many students feels study is so hard and difficult. There are various different reasons that might play the vital role in making students lazy and inactive as far as the study concerned, but few of the reasons which are considered to be significant and most crucial one are being listed as:-

1. The first reason of being lazy in during the studies is the incomplete sleep, if the students are not taking the proper sleep during the night they will always feel lazy & dizzy while their studies. Many students are stuck in game or addicted the internet (WhatsApp, Facebook etc.). They are awake all night online, chats, surf Facebook or do something else related the internet. Academics is a mental activity so it require the freshness of the mind which is mainly achieved after proper sleep and once the sleep is not being taken properly then the laziness will prevail during the studies.

2. The second reason is that many students never think about future, plus they are involved in too many activities and having too much fun. Seventy percent of total students don't know what they are studying for; fifty present students don't know what they will do in future; and most of students have no aim of life. Those are reasons they don't do efforts to study hard. They are lazy and rely on their parents.

3. The third one is the specially which they are pursuing is not in line with their interest, hobbies and dream. Therefore they are feeling boring and uncomfortable on studying it.Many students go school/college because of their parents request, don't because they like it.Almost people don't want to be obliged ;they want to do what they like. So

some students are lazy in studying subjects that they hate or don't like to easy to understand.

4. The fourth and most important things is the social media. Social media can be good and bad thing, it is resourceful in some ways but it can also be negative, if you spend all your working hours checking, scrolling, looking on social media. Do you know how many social media platforms are there? Quite a few and they are only growing we have facebook,whattsapp, Instagram and more are evolving.

   Lazy people start to see less of their friends and family and instead just lived through social media. This is actually one of the very common habit of lazy person especially with social media being so huge nowdays. Social media platform allow people to check their notification every minute, engage in meaningless debates and conversation.

5. Another habit of a lazy person is never wanting to learn anything new as they are perfectly with where they stand and what they already know. This is definitely not good habit as it is good to learn new things and embrace the unknown. Lazy people tend to avoid the gaining of knowledge, experience or even spiritual growth. Perhaps it the fear or may be the result back to when they were in school and forced to do all activities they when they really wanted to play outside. and now they

are older they have become lazy in their efforts in their learning.

## How to Overcome Laziness of a Student

One of the things a student experiences, whether s/he's already having a master's degree or still a fifth grader, is the struggle in overcoming laziness in studying. It is the time when you have tons of school works to do yet you don't feel like doing it. Laziness keeps us from doing important tasks and it could hinder our studies. If it continues, it will become a habit that could have a negative implication to your grades or worst to your future endeavours. Sounds horrible right? But then, just like any other things, you can get rid of it. Here are some tips that could help you overcome laziness in studying:

## Be in a comfortable place

One thing that could help fight laziness is finding a good location. Being in a comfortable place whether it's in your favourite library, or just in your own bedroom that is free from distractions could help you to relax your mind and focus on studying.

## Make a study plan

Having a study plan will help you organize and track down your tasks easier. Make a timetable wherein you set a time schedule for a certain subject and other tasks to do. List down your assignments that are due and arrange them like a calendar. In this way, it could help you prioritize and get it done on time.

## Take one step at a time

Taking actions one step at a time will help you beat laziness. Breaking down bigger tasks into smaller tasks will help you avoid being stressed. This will make your tasks a lot more manageable. Completing a sub task will serve as a motivation for you to continue other sub tasks thus, helping you finish your overall task in a more convenient way.

## Make a to-do list

There are times that because of so much things to do, just like preparing for major exams, you lost track of other things that need to be done. You could make a to-do list with just a piece of sticky note since it's handy and you could place it anywhere. Placing a to-do list where you could see it every time, will help you remind what to do next. Also, making a to-do list will help you focus on doing your tasks especially that distractions are just around the corner.

## Remove all distractions

Being distracted while studying will make you lazier. It is better to get rid of all distractions such as turning off your TV or internet connection or just by simply switching your phone to silent mode or you could even ask your roommate or family member to give you privacy. Keep in mind that avoiding these disturbances will aid you to concentrate and study effectively.

## Find motivation

One of the top reasons why many students are lazy to study is due to lack of motivation. Finding motivation will help you to concentrate and think about the benefits after studying, just like passing an exam and getting high grades or recognition from your teacher or you will be noticed by the cutie you have a crush on when you got the perfect score. Visualize yourself after studying and think of its positive outcome. In this way you could study effectively since you already have that will to achieve something.

## Think about its consequences

Thinking about the positive outcome of studying could be a motivation for a person to start studying. If you have this kind of motivation in your mind, yet you still do not have that willpower to start it and laziness still dominates you, how about trying the other way around? Instead of thinking the benefits of studying, think about the consequences if you don't study. You could possibly have a failing grade and will be forced to take up the same subject again. It sounds terrible. So have this as a motivation to get up, flip the pages of your notebooks, start reading and learning.

## Do easier tasks first

One thing that could be a problem in studying, is actually how to start it. You tend to be overwhelmed with bigger tasks and how to start it and finish it on time. Take it easy. Don't put too much pressure on yourself as it could add up to your laziness. That feeling when you want to give up even though you are not yet beginning. Overcome it by starting with easier tasks. For example, start to study topics on a certain subject that is easier for you. Once you successfully completed studying that topic, you will have the confidence to move on to more difficult ones.

## Discipline yourself

This is the most important thing. The key to beat your laziness is to discipline yourself. In order to achieve something successfully, you must need to stop certain habits or behaviours. As with studying, you must need to stop certain things that could distract you and lose your focus and start doing things that could contribute to accomplish good results. If you easily get distracted with gadgets, put them away while you are studying. Make this a habit so that the next time you have to study, you will get used to it. Keep in mind that these little sacrifices will have great results in the future.

## Reward yourself

Overcoming laziness is really a struggle, so every time you manage to do it, have yourself a reward. Like if you study for 20 minutes or finish an assignment without any interruptions, give yourself a treat, whether it is your favourite bar of chocolate or favourite ice cream. This will help you build a mindset that making efforts results into positive outcomes.

Being lazy with studying is a normal thing. Everyone experiences it, especially if there are a lot to study on and you don't know where and how to start. However, whether it is for a major exam or a small quiz, you have to take it seriously. Commit yourself to break the habit of laziness. Work harder! Keep in mind that the harder you try, the greater the result is.

# Seven

## True Friend

Friends plays an vital role in a every person's life. Friends can be so important if they are right/true friends. Friends play an very important role in student's life. Basically in most of the students life's are made or destroyed by the means of friends. It says that the way I act will determine the type of people I will attract to be my friends.

True friends are people who make the life easy and entertaining. In true friendship, it should be strictly honest, loyal, and chaste in every action. Perhaps it is word commitment that unlocks the real meaning of friendship. True friends are wonderful. They encourage when one is sad, they entertain when one is lonesome, and they listen when one has problems.

There are varieties of friends, co-workers, social workers, schoolmates, and much more. But our school time friends are very memorable. Each type of friends are helpful in one way or the other. Co-workers could help solve problems and stress gain in the workplace. Friends from the community widen one's prospective by introducing new people from different areas. Friends that grew up with or schoolmate would share the happiness and sadness one might has. However, friends that grew up with might not always be the best friends because they could be faking it or been concealing some secrets. So, it is very important for one to recognize all the friends she/he has because good friends are hard to find. Student should be alert to choose a friend.

# GOOD FRIENDS
care for each other..
# CLOSE FRIENDS
understand each other, But
# True Friends
Stay forever..
beyond words,
beyond distance,
beyond time....!

A true friend shows right way but a bad friend will be the cause of their destroyed life. You mostly listen avoid bad company but it is medotory to select a good company. There is a very important role of friendship in student's life. A true friend helps you in your personal growth and development. True friends should not be measured only on the base on the time spent together. With good friends, one is able to have a more meaningful life. It is very difficult to have a definition of a good friend for everyone to agree upon. Since everyone has different personalities, friends are one look for could be very different. Nonetheless, there are some common characteristics shared among most of the definitions. The three main qualities that define a good true friend are loyalty, understanding, and encouraging.

Choose friends who share your values so you can strengthen and encourage each other in living high standards.

- To have a good friend to be a good friend.
- As you seek to be a friend to others, don't compromise your standards.
- Give your hand with sympathy.
- Only your true friend told you your weakness which you avoid.
- You should share your happiness and sorrows.

Loyalty is one of the main quality one looks for when searching for true friends. Trusts are gain by having trustworthy friends. At least once in a person's life, one would encounter a friend that likes to share secrets that belong to others with his/her friends. This could be very entertaining for his/her friends, yet the person with the secret would feel irritated. With no doubts, one would not desire to have a blabbermouth person as a friend; except one wants to spread rumours around or wants to find out other people's secrets. So, it would be most comfortable to tell secrets to someone who is trustworthy. A loyal friend is hard to meet in today's society.

In the context of social media, the term "friend" is often used to describe *contacts* rather than *relationships*. You have the ability to send your "friends" a message, but this is not the same thing as having a relationship with a person one on one.

True friends influence those with whom they associates to "rise a little higher be little better" You can help another particular young man, prepare for and serve honourable missions. You can help remain morally clean. Your righteous influence and friends can have an eternal effect not only on the lives of those with whom you associates but also generation to come.

A true friend in is someone who is kind, friendly, and the kind of person who wants to be involved with activities that are spiritual, clean, and fun, but not bad or any mentally distracted activities. We all need to be careful of what kind of friend we chose to have. If we have friends who just want to be friend because of your stuff or money, then that is not being a good friend. Your friend should not have non-productive gossips, or want or talk about inappropriate things. Being a good friend will make others want to do the same. It is always said that the way I act will determine the type of people I will attract to be my friends. He/She also says that the only way to have friends it to be one. I think that is true because we have to be friends before we can make them. As we are friendly to those around us and try to be good examples, the people around us will try to keep their standards up because we do.

## Role of a true friend in individual's life

**Self-Awareness** – *A Story The grass-eating Tiger.*

It's about a pregnant Tigress who goes out hunting one day. She finds a whole herd of goats. She goes after the goats because she is very, very hungry. She is ravenous. So she attacks them desperately, and she gets so tired and runs so hard that she collapses in exhaustion and she dies giving birth to her cub.

When the goats return to the field, they find the motherless new born. Those goats decide to adopt him. So he grows up repeating behaviours' like those around him. He bleats. He eats grass. He believes himself to be a goat.

So this little cub who grows into a tiger now is wandering with the goats and acting like a goat and bleating like the goats and eating the way the goats eat.

Then one day a tiger, a big male tiger, comes into the goat herd and all the goats scatter except this little tiger. He is about a year old now and looking at this big male tiger somehow he is sensing an affinity with this tiger. But he freezes in his tracks and he stands there staring at the tiger.

The big tiger comes over to him and says 'What's wrong with you?' The little one says 'What do you mean what's wrong with me?' The big tiger says 'What's wrong with you? What are you doing? You are acting weird.

You are acting like a goat.' The little tiger says 'I am a goat!' The big one says 'No you're not. You are not a goat.' He leads the little tiger over to a pond.

A very still pond. He said 'Now look at yourself. Really look at yourself.' The little cub looks at himself, and he looks at the big tiger, and he is confused. The tiger says 'Come with me.' He takes him back to his den, and in the den, there is some leftover meat from a gazelle that had been his recent kill.

So he says to the little tiger 'Eat this.' The little cub says 'Well no way. I am a vegetarian. ' The tiger says 'Try it. Just try it.' So the little tiger reaches over and he takes a bite off the bone.

In this Hindu story, when that little tiger who thought he was a goat reaches down and tastes some of the meat, at first, he chokes on the meat. He gags and then a piece of that meat enters his bloodstream, and the cub begins to stretch.

He bares his claws, he opens his mouth wide, and he lets out for the very first time in his life a small roar.

That first roar isn't very fearsome. It's not yet all the roar that the tiger will give, but that first roar is called the roar of awakening. It's the first moment when this being recognized that he wasn't who he thought himself to be.

He wasn't limited to the kind of life he had been living and that there was way more for him. And so it is for every one of us.

There is something very powerful in the shifting of your self- image from a personality with your history driven understanding about who you are to a conscious, aware understanding of yourself, your **Self-Awareness.**

What is the theme of the story is "In real the big tiger is the true friend of grass eating tiger as he inspired him that you are a tiger not a goat so live like tiger. Big tiger plays a role of a true friend."

## What for friends

Intent is far more important than content. A child may buy a gift for its parents from the very same pocket money the dad given to him. But the intent of the child is selfless, it is still feels like a gift when they take it into their hands. In contrast, a free gift from an elder would appears as crush when perceived to have vested interests attached.

The greatest and noblest leaders of society have always been straight and forthright in their speeches, policies and activities. The leaders were not orators, but people, who spoke with simple words. They are not handsome, rich, or beautiful. But the people listened to them; followed them. Nay, they scarified their lives for them. It's not money, fame or power most people really want. Deep inside, what they actually crave is a sheltering friendship. Henry Ford said, " I have been surrounded not by real friends but people who are interested only in my money. If by giving away all wealth, I could acquire a single friends, I would do it".

A true friend, one never deserts you. One who is always there when you need him. One who defends, protects, and forgives you even when you are wrong. That is true friend. It is so wonderful to have such a friends. He or she might be in the form of parents, fellow sibling, relative, colleague, good book or guru or teachers. But a good friend is someone everyone needs.

These friends tell you the bitter truth, but it's easy for you to swallow it because you know their intent is pure. You know they are not using the truth to pull you down or hurt you like others do. You know they are using it to pull you up and heal you, like no one else does. Such friends don't have a political agenda in their lives. Unlike today's leader's leaders who have 'no permanent relationships, but only permanent interests, true friends have eternal unflinching plans for you. Therefore I shall liberate you of even the tiniest of flaws. This is my deepest pledge to you " True friends push us towards perfection". Friends are committed, determined. They you before themselves ! They appreciate you more than the whole world put together. They know to you through to your bones. They understand every beat of your heart and every frequency of the thought waves in your brain. They comprehend the agonies of your soul and ecstasy of your dreams. Yet they manage to handle them all; controlling your tantrums, calming your nerves and cradling your soul. Isn't this what most people want? Someone to soothe them and assure them everything will be all right in the end ?.

But such friends are so rare! And only true spiritual mentors live on forever. Parents, spouse and friends pass away. Fellow siblings purse career in far off lands.

A feeling of loneliness and defencelessness descends on people- however rich or powerful they may be -when they begin to lose their nearest and dearest. But this is life's trademark. In fact, life is debacle.

We can't prevent our closest ones from leaving us alone in this harsh, wild world. But their intent in leaving us is pure too; they are nudging us to take their place as selfless friend and guardian of someone else! We must follow their footsteps and tread their path. As they were unto, we must be unto others. But remember, even if you can't be as helpful as the friend who helped and guided you, you can still bear his essential qualities; a pure pristine intention. Most of us will never go to great things, but we can all do small things in this great selfless way !

## Sings of true friend

In today's world of instant online connections and accumulating thousands of friends on social media platforms, discerning between virtual friends and "real" friends can become quite a challenge. Most of the time, the people we meet online simply don't get us like the friends we have in our real lives, they just haven't been there through the tough times, and don't know our background. Now, that isn't to say that you can't become close with people you meet online or in other non-traditional ways, but usually, we have one or two close friends that we know have our backs no matter what.

# Do You Know Who are Your True Friends? These Signs Will Help You...

### *They Always With You in Good or Bad Time*

A true friend would never leave you just because you're going through a rough patch. They would stick by your side and help you through the darkness. A clear sign of a true friend is that he or she will laugh with you during the great times, and cry with you during the bad ones. In today's world of flaky, fake friendships, cherish those who aren't just fair-weather friends. These are the people you will want to keep in your life, as they are definitely genuine friends who want the best for you and care about your well-being.

### *They Accept You Exactly As You Are*

In our list of signs of a true friend, we couldn't skip over the fact that a real friend will allow you to be whoever you want to be, without judgment. True friends don't ask you to change the parts of yourself that even you can't accept – they embrace you anyway, flaws and all. They put your insecurities to rest, and actually find beauty in your imperfections. A true friend will love and adore you for whatever you identify with, and will admire you for both your strengths and weaknesses.

True friends don't place conditions on your friendships – they let you come as you are, and don't put any pressure on you or the relationship.

### They Will Always With Your Struggle

A true friend will not just let you go through tough times alone – they will drop whatever they're doing to assist you in hard times. True friends don't just leave those they love out in the cold; they pick them up off the ground, dust them off, and carry them back to safety once again. A true friend understands that you can't possibly deal with all of life's trials and tribulations by yourself, so they have your back no matter what.

### They Have Time For You

Real friends never blow you off or tell you they're too busy to see you. While they might have to rear range their schedule a bit, a true friend will never use lack of time or energy as an excuse to avoid hanging out. A clear sign of a true friend is that they always seem to follow through with their promises and see you no matter how busy their life gets.

They don't allow life to take over and just toss you aside when things get hectic for them; they include you in their life, and set aside specific times each week to catch up with you.

### *You Feel Totally Comfortable Around Them*

Another sign of a true friendship is that both of you can feel at ease around one another. You don't have to fake a laugh or force conversation; things just seem to flow effortlessly between you two, and you wouldn't have it any other way. A true friend doesn't make you feel uncomfortable or scared to open up; real friends open their arms and hearts to you, and put down their walls to let you in.

You can tell each other anything and not have to censor yourselves; after all, what would friendship be if you constantly had to monitor the things you say? A real friend would never want you to hold back your thoughts and feelings, and encourage you to share whatever is on your mind. You can act silly and let your guard down, and not have to think twice about doing so. If you want to read more about signs of an authentic friendship, you can do so here.

*It's beginning...*

www.ingramcontent.com/pod-product-compliance
Lightning Source LLC
Chambersburg PA
CBHW051833130726
47987CB00002B/522